"If you aspire to be really interesting rea~~d~~
Chris Cramer, former Presiden~~t~~   ᶜ CNN
International

"Engrossing, abs~~o~~
Major General A   ~~ᵢ~~al Royal
Marines

"These guys understan~~d~~   ~~t~~ings of how to be interesting. Dave and
Mark lift the lid on the s~~   ~~nd give you, the reader,the tools to change
your life. They worked wo~~n~~ders for mine!"

Steve (Interesting) Davis, snooker legend

"As the Chinese proverb says – 'May we live in interesting times' – this book
lets us do exactly that."

Mike Southon, author *The Beermat Entrepreneur*

Cover design: Mackerel Ltd

© 2013 David Gillespie and Mark Warren

Registered office

Capstone Publishing Ltd. (A Wiley Company), John Wiley and Sons Ltd, The Atrium, Southern Gate, Chichester, West Sussex, PO19 8SQ, United Kingdom

For details of our global editorial offices, for customer services and for information about how to apply for permission to reuse the copyright material in this book please see our website at www.wiley.com.

The right of the author to be identified as the author of this work has been asserted in accordance with the Copyright, Designs and Patents Act 1988.

Reprinted June 2013, September 2013, November 2015

Wiley publishes in a variety of print and electronic formats and by print-on-demand. Some material included with standard print versions of this book may not be included in e-books or in print-on-demand. If this book refers to media such as a CD or DVD that is not included in the version you purchased, you may download this material at http://booksupport.wiley.com. For more information about Wiley products, visit www.wiley.com.

Library of Congress Cataloging-in-Publication Data is available

Gillespie, David, 1958-
    How to be interesting : simple ways to increase your personal appeal / David Gillespie, Mark Warren.
      pages cm
    ISBN 978-0-85708-406-4 (pbk.) – ISBN 978-0-85708-405-7 (ebk.) –
    ISBN 978-0-85708-404-0 (ebk.) – ISBN 978-0-85708-403-3 (ebk.)   1. Charisma
(Personality trait)   2. Self-actualization (Psychology)   I. Warren, Mark, 1958-   II. Title.
    BF698.35.C45G55 2013
    158.2–dc23
                            2013001465

A catalogue record for this book is available from the British Library.

ISBN 978-0-857-08406-4 (pbk) ISBN 978-0-857-08405-7 (ebk)
ISBN 978-0-857-08404-0 (ebk) ISBN 978-0-857-08403-3 (ebk)

Designed by Andy Prior Design
Set in 8pt ITC Stone Serif Std
Printed in Great Britain by TJ International Ltd, Padstow, Cornwall, UK

gripping
dull
compulsive
thought-provoking
amusing
environment
pleasing
intriguing
riveting
beguiling
tedious
attractive
engaging
mind-numbing
entrancing
compelling
absorbing
boring
curious
entertaining
engrossing
different

HOW TO BE spellbinding
unusual

interesting

enthralling
uninteresting
stimulating
stirring
tiresome
fascinating
appealing

by David Gillespie and Mark Warren

CAPSTONE

A book to make you think

How to be interesting?

This is not an instruction manual. This is not a book that will tell you what to do. It's a book that will make you think.

This is a book that asks questions, in what we hope is a thought-provoking study on what it is to "be interesting".

It will also give some answers.

You will notice that the words HOW TO BE in the book title are small compared to the word INTERESTING. That's why.

If you've picked up this book hoping that it will instruct you on how to be interesting in seven easy steps, or five tough challenges, we are sorry. Please put the book back on the shelf and save yourself some money.

What this book will do is:

☺ Give you some insight into what makes people interesting.

☺ Give you space and time to think about how interesting you are ...or could be.

Interested? Read on...

David Gillespie is an actor, voice-over artist, keynote speaker and communications expert.

He was born in Nottingham and moved to London to train as an actor at The Webber Douglas Academy of Dramatic Art.

After graduating he joined the company of the Theatre Royal Stratford East where he "cut his teeth" as a performer in the theatre's many Variety Nights, appearing in sketches with comedy greats like Barry Cryer, John Junkin and Victor Spinnetti. He has since appeared on stage in London's West End and in theatres throughout the world.

David's many TV and film credits include *EastEnders, Red Dwarf, Love, Honour and Obey, Bedtime, Sensitive Skin, Roman Mysteries, Stuck, Who gets the Dog, The Wee Man* and more. Dave played the brilliant character DI Beach in the totally improvised fly-on-the-wall, cult comedy series *Operation Good Guys*. It won a Silver Rose and Prix de la Presse at Montreux.

As co-founder of The Speechworks (www.thespeechworks.co.uk), his seminars on communication skills have been enjoyed by many organizations across the world. These include AOL, Apple, Bacardi, BNP Paribas, Comic Relief, Google, ICAEW, Toshiba and many others.

David is often interviewed as a communications expert. He has appeared on BBC radio, BBC Worldwide News and Newsnight to comment on the communication skills of political leaders.

Mark Warren was born in Bridport, Dorset where he attended St Catherine's Primary School and Colfox School.

He has a BSc. in Medical Biochemisty from Royal Holloway College, University of London and a PGCE from Chelsea College, University of London.

He is a script writer, copywriter and creative director who works in broadcast media, advertising/marketing and digital communication channels.

As an award-winning copywriter, he has created advertising and marketing campaigns for some of the world's leading agency groups.

His television scriptwriting credits include comedy dramas and comedies for Aardman Animation, Baby Cow Productions, Tiger Aspect, BBC1, BBC4, Spitting Image, Sky Atlantic and others. Mark was a writer on *Lenny Henry in Pieces*, which won a Golden Rose of Montreux.

Just some of the actors he has worked with include Alison Steadman, Charles Dance, Amelia Bullmore, Hugo Speer, Samuel Anderson, Omid Djalili, Harry Enfield, Lenny Henry, Basil Brush and Dave Gillespie.

Website content creation credits include *The Sopranos* and *Engineering an Empire* for A&E network and others.

He is the co-creator and writer of the *Celeb* cartoon strip in *Private Eye* magazine, with the artist Charles Peattie. Together they are authors of the book, *Celeb. The Original Gary Bloke from Private Eye.*

With David Gillespie he is a co-founder of The Speechworks (www.thespeechworks. co.uk), a select group of performance-based professionals and leaders in communication skills and presentation skills training. Their clients range from blue-chip corporates, professional bodies and start-ups to SMES, charities and public figures.

Contents page

You say you're looking for an interesting man... mmm, might struggle with that one
FIND U ONE DATING AGENCY

Why do you want to be interesting?

Not a daft question. It has to be one of the basic human needs. In order to survive on a daily basis you have to have the attention of someone and on some days a lot of people. This is purely functional but the need seems to go beyond that. Why do you want people to take an interest in you? Do you actually need them to? We think so.

We crave the company of other people for security, protection, companionship, comfort, entertainment and sex. It stops us going mad. We want to be interesting to others for many reasons. Socially it's important for us to be interesting in order not to be left out and ignored. Domestically we want to be interesting for some of the more basic reasons of love and comfort. In business we want to be interesting to our colleagues and be part of the team, to our clients so they continue doing business with us and to our superiors so we are not overlooked when it comes to promotion and pay rises. Being of interest for most people is a primary requirement for wellbeing.

Being talked about can also make us feel interesting.

> "There's only one thing worse than being talked about and that's not being talked about."
>
> **Oscar Wilde**

When you have the interest of others it means that you have a good chance of being stimulated in one way or another.

So what do we mean by interesting?

It is an interesting word, interesting. What does it actually mean?

The Oxford English Dictionary definition:

1) that concerns, touches, affects or is of importance, important.

2) adapted to excite interest, having the qualities that rouse curiosity, engage attention, or appeal to the emotion of interest.

3) to be in an interesting condition – pregnant.

Causing curiosity; holding the attention

Interested
Concerned, affected, having an interest, concern, or share in something.

Interest

n. attention, attentiveness, care, commitment, concern, curiosity, involvement, notice, regard. scrutiny.

v. absorb, appeal to, arouse the curiosity of, attract, capture the imagination, captivate, concern, divert, enchant, engage, engross, entertain, enthral, fascinate, intrigue, involve, occupy, preoccupy, stimulate, turn on, excite.

Maybe pinning down what interesting is, isn't as easy and straightforward as we thought ...

(interest someone in)
persuade someone to undertake or acquire (something)

The state of wanting to know or learn about something or someone.

Interesting – absorbing, appealing, attracting, challenging, compelling, curious, engaging, engrossing, entertaining, fascinating, gripping, riveting, imaginative, intriguing, inviting, original, piquant.

Interesting
in 11 other languages

Interesa – Esperanto

Interessante – Afrikaans

Ddiddorol – Welsh

Ilginç – Turkish

Interesgarria – Basque

Interessanti – Maltese

Enteresan – Haitian Creole

Kuvutia – Swahili

ויינעמ – Hebrew

Suimiúil – Irish

Daj – Klingon

It seems that "interesting" and "being" are very closely linked…

The Latin verb, interesse = "to concern, to be of importance"
inter + esse = "between" + "be"

Esse = "to be"
↓
English word essence or the being of something.

INTERESTING

compelling
unusual
curious
inviting
imaginative
piquant
appealing
important
arresting
attracting
immersing
thrilling
alluring
electrifying
engrossing
charming
captivating
gripping
enchanting
interest
fascinating
stimulating
exciting
diverting
riveting
interestingness
entertaining
absorbing
amusing
newsworthy
intriguing

4

INT,STUDY.DAY

Dave and Mark sit at a desk. They are thinking about
material for the book they've been commissioned to write.
Dave is looking at the *Oxford English Dictionary*. Mark is
looking at some notes.

> DAVE
>
> It's an interesting word, interesting, isn't it?

> MARK
>
> Yeah.

> DAVE
>
> And it's interesting that people find
> it "interesting" when we ask them what the
> word interesting means to them.

> MARK
>
> Yes … you've just given me an idea. There's one
> thing we must be sure to do when we come to write
> this book though.

> DAVE
>
> What's that then?

> MARK
>
> We must avoid the overuse of the word interesting
> in an intentionally "interesting" way.

> DAVE
>
> Absolutely. If we over use the word interesting it
> won't be interesting will it?

> MARK
>
> No. It'll be boring.

What is the opposite of interesting?

The opposite of interesting? Well, that would be boring. So what is a bore? The old adage would have us believe that "a bore is someone who talks about themselves when you want to talk about yourself".

Do you remember the last time you spoke to someone who bored you? Or worse still, the last time you spoke to someone and noticed him or her glazing over? How did it make you feel? Not good. We all want to be appreciated and thought interesting. It's human nature, plain and simple.

A bore could also be deemed as someone who has no apparent interest in anyone or anything – or who has no significant contribution to interactive situations.

There are, however, certain people who do not say or contribute very much in social situations but still generate interest. This could be because of a certain look, demeanour or aura, which might be an interesting contribution in itself but how long does that last?

People we think of as boring are generally people we wish to get away from. Is it easy to spot a bore? They might be the person who nobody is talking to. They might also be the person who is holding court to a collection of very disinterested faces.

Do boring people attract other boring people and stick together? Do boring people find themselves very interesting and assume that everyone else does too? Hmmm ... but just as interesting can be different things to different people, boring can be the same. This is why it is not easy to generalize about whom and what is boring.

If we do not want to be thought of as boring should we take more interest in other people?

So who's the bore now?

"Develop interest in life as you see it; in people, things, literature, music – the world is so rich, simply throbbing with rich treasures, beautiful souls and interesting people. Forget yourself."

Henry Miller

Bored or boring?

Let's take a look at boredom through the ages ...

I'm bored Mummy.

A lot of young children become bored quite easily. They have little knowledge or experience of life. They need to be continually stimulated – vocally, visually and aurally. Vivid, interesting objects are of huge benefit. Interesting stuff helps you grow. That's how you learn and develop when you are young. The more children know, the less bored they become. The less bored they are, the more interested and more interesting they become.

This is soooo boring!

The Kevin and Perry sketch on the *Harry Enfield Show* caught the moody teenage attitude to life brilliantly well. All adults, everything they do and everything they ask their children to do, are "sooooo boring!" How many times can we remember ourselves as teenagers saying "there's nothing to do ...I'm bored!" It's that wonderful period between knowing everything there is to know, and being an adult. It's excusable – we've all done it. Being a bored teenager is part of growing up.

I have a really low boredom threshold.

Now, here's the rub. Boredom in adulthood. Are people who say that they are bored interesting people? Do we want to find out why they are bored? Can we be bothered? Why do people crave the interest of others by boasting that they have a low boredom threshold? Is it to make themselves sound intelligent – even interesting?

> "I drink to make other people more interesting."
>
> **Ernest Hemingway**

I'm not interesting, I'm ordinary

"I'm not interesting, I'm ordinary. I live an ordinary sort of life and do a very ordinary job. To be interesting surely you have to do something out of the ordinary or extraordinary?"

Yours humbly,

Only Me

Dear Only Me,

You're wrong – everyone has the potential to be interesting. And this book will hopefully help you see that. Of course people's achievements and accomplishments help to make them interesting. But that doesn't mean you have to be capable of doing amazing things if you are to be interesting to others.

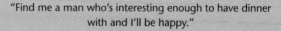

Climbing Mount Everest or winning an Olympic gold medal would naturally make someone seem interesting. Why? Because we would know all about their fantastic achievement and would be curious to find out more about their success. How? Why? What was it like?

But seeming interesting wouldn't necessarily make them interesting. We've all met very successful people who aren't interesting in the slightest.

Sometimes this is because they're not interested in you or anyone else for that matter. Or sometimes the Great Achievers have let their success go to their head and now think that they are better than the rest of us.

You don't have to be a celebrity, super-successful or to have done something incredible to be interesting. It is just as much about who you are as it is about what you have done.

Remember, achievements are all relative. What makes for the more compelling story?

The arrogant, aloof millionaire footballer who has just bought a second mansion?

Or the mother of a disabled child who walks across Africa to raise money for children's charities?

Which would you like to get to know better? Which story do you think would be the more interesting?

We continually achieve things that make us interesting – they don't have to be earth-shattering milestones. Every little thing we do gives us experience, insight and knowledge. And these give us more stories to tell and help define us as individuals.

The world's most boring person

Imagine this scenario. Someone, let's call them A. Bore (the A could be Ann or Adrian), decides that he or she is so boring that they decide to try and get voted as the world's most boring person. There's reference to the most interesting man in the world elsewhere in the book btw.

They are determined to earn this accolade. They set up the awards and invite people to enter the competition. They select judges and choose a tedious prize. They have a very boring awards ceremony, which is held somewhere very boring. Maybe either the town Boring☺ in Oregon, USA or the hamlet of Dull in Perthshire, Scotland. Dull and Boring actually exist and have voted to become "sister communities" we're told.

Back to our story. A. Bore wins the award and is crowned The World's Most Boring Person. As soon as the bore wins the award, he or she is no longer boring because they have achieved something and have an interesting story to tell. In fact, you could argue that as soon as A. Bore decided to set off on the quest, they ceased to be boring and became interesting.

☺ *Boring was named after an early resident, William Boring.*

What makes people interesting?

The *How to be Interesting* survey

We wanted to find out what the word interesting meant to people and what their thoughts were about the whole area of what makes someone interesting.

Using social media, email and our personal contacts we sent out this simple survey. The target group was chosen to reflect a wide cross-section of society by social background and age (from 18 to 80). The balance by sex of the survey group was about a 50/50 male/female split.

The feedback was great and the answers thought-provoking. Some answers were careful and well considered, some were quick, off-the-top-of-the head responses and a very small number just plain silly.

What does the word "interesting" mean to you?

What do you think makes someone interesting? / What is your definition of an interesting person? 😁

Why is it good to be interesting?

 Whoever answered "big breasts" deserves a special award for "wit and wisdom". Not!

Anything which adds to your knowledge in something you find inspiring.

Having my interest piqued, being intrigued.

Something away from the norm.

Standing out.

What does the word "interesting" mean to you?

Something fascinating if the subject matter appeals to me, and conversely, something boring if it does not.

Curiosity.

Someone who challenges your views and opinions.

Either something new or a new way of looking at the familiar.

Being outside of the normal range!

Something or someone who makes you rethink your view.

Something that brings new ideas or thoughts, be it a person, place or object.

Being mildly intrigued to full-on obsession.

Wanting to find out more.

Different, new, layered.

Something that captures the imagination, different from the norm or what you may expect.

Captures your attention and makes you take note/listen.

Something or someone who catches your attention and is absorbing.

Experience, and if they can bring insight with that experience.

People who are interested are generally interesting. Enthusiasm is infectious.

If they are amusing, engaging, unusual.

Thoughtful, curious and adventurous.

Someone with good stories.

What do you think makes someone interesting? / What is your definition of an interesting person?

Common interests – shared values.

Wisdom. Stories.

Someone with insight into the human condition and who takes a position on things and can explain their take on those things.

Someone who excites my mind and can get my attention and keep it.

Someone who is still memorable one week after meeting.

Someone whose ideas and doctrines bear scrutiny.

When you want to listen to them. When you want to know more. Something that grabs your attention.

A person with a depth of knowledge who knows things which capture my attention.

Someone who you are drawn towards, or you can learn something from.

Charisma and intelligence when combined together.

Someone who makes you feel at ease instantly and is engaging with a sense of humour.

Someone who has done something, which you find impressive or significant.

Someone who sees the world in a different way, so that even when they talk about ordinary things it is interesting.

Passions for travel, sport, culture etc. and a sense of humour that's their own.

Their life story and experiences. Them sharing information.

Personality – quirkiness, joviality, fun, humour, behaviour/ attitude, appearance, language, intellect, opinions/views.

Those with an interest in things outside of their own life.

17

It helps keep knowledge and experience growing and developing. Without interesting, collective enterprise would stop!

"Interesting people" can spark/draw out other people to be more "interesting".

Adds character and depth of personality.

It is better than being boring and surrounding yourself with a lot of bores.

Why is it good to be interesting?

Makes people sit up and take notice.

Beauty fades and beyond physical pleasure it is the best pleasure there is – that sense of complete immersion in something ... almost trance-like ... the joy of sharing an interest in a subject is profound.

You make an impact – win friends, lovers, job interviews, success in your chosen career.

It's how we grow and enable others to grow.

I think if you're interesting you're often interested. These are two big parts of life for social creatures like humans.

No one wants to be thought of as boring do they? Look for new ideas and experiences as you go through life and it will stay interesting.

It is closely linked to charisma. People will want to spend time with you; you might leave them feeling different about something or with a new perspective.

Richer life experience. Stronger connections. Inner strength.

Everybody is interesting in different ways.

You make an impression and people remember you.

You always have friends and company and people gravitate towards you.

It's smart to be interesting so that people will want to talk to you and hear what you have to say.

Communication is paramount. If someone or something isn't interesting, we disengage, switch off – and that feels uncomfortable

If we keep asking questions, continuous improvement is the only way.

Helps people keep interested, which makes for a far better social group.

It's all about being interested in new possibilities.

The world would be boring if everyone was dull!

Our survey says...

There were three main conclusions we drew from the answers.

Being interesting ...
or an interesting person ...

...
is, not
surprisingly,
something that
almost everyone
thought was a good
thing.

... means different things to
different people.

... throws up common themes – being
interested in others, being curious,
communication, sharing experiences,
knowledge ...

Be a **sponge,**
absorb
knowledge

What's the point of knowledge?

What's the point of thinking or understanding?

Let's take the word philosophy as a starting point. It comes from the Greek word *philosophia*, the literal meaning of which is "love of wisdom".

Wikipedia describes wisdom thus:

Wisdom is a deep
understanding and realization
of people, things, events or situations,
resulting in the ability to apply perceptions,
judgments and actions in keeping with this
understanding.

WISDOM

It often requires control of one's emotional reactions
so that universal principles, reason and knowledge
prevail to determine one's actions. Wisdom is also
the comprehension of what is true coupled
with optimum judgment as to action.
Synonyms include: sagacity,
discernment, or insight.

Note the use of the word insight. For us, in simple terms, wisdom is about making use of knowledge. It is knowledge about the world around us, knowledge about the people around us and knowledge about ourselves.

Acquire knowledge whenever you can. And actively share it with others – with a passion. That's a great way to be interesting.

If knowledge and sharing it helps people be interesting, has Wikipedia helped the world "be interesting"? Absolutely.

Jimmy Wales said that his original concept was to provide a free encyclopedia for every single person in the world. He had the vision to imagine a world in which every single person on the planet is given free access to the sum of all human knowledge.

It's no wonder that he once described himself as very much an enlightenment kind of guy.

In some ways, in this digital, technological and information revolution that's hurtling forward, we are living through another age of enlightenment.

As Jimmy once said, "I just get up every day and do what seems like the most interesting, fun thing to do".

"To acquire knowledge one must study: but to acquire wisdom one must observe."

Marilyn vos Savant

Columnist who was given the Guinness World Record for Highest IQ (Women) in 1985 with an IQ score of 190.

Wikipedia

Here's some interesting stuff about Wikipedia – correct at the time of writing.

- Wikipedia was launched in January 2001 by Jimmy Wales and Larry Sanger. So it's only just 12 years old.

- Wiki comes from the Hawaiian word meaning "quick".

- All the articles have been written collaboratively by volunteers across the world. Almost all of them can be edited by anyone with access to the site.

- There are about 100 000 active contributors, editions in 285 languages and an estimated 365 million readers worldwide.

- There are Wikipedias in Cheyenne and other indigenous languages of the Americas.

- Wikipedia has a list of "deleted articles with freaky titles" called DAFT.

- There's a competition to guess what the last article to appear in Wikipedia will be.

- There's a Facebook page called "searching yourself on the internet hoping you have a Wikipedia page :))."   At the time of writing it has just six likes.

Life without enquiry

Ah, Socrates. (Not the Brazilian footballer whose full name was Sócrates Brasileiro Sampaio de Souza Vieira de Oliveira and was also a qualified doctor by the way).

Socrates is credited for laying the foundation for Western Philosophy. He devoted much of his life to thinking about how we, as humans, ought to live. He also believed that wisdom begins with wonder.

"I know one thing, that I know nothing."

Socrates left no writings of his own but is quoted and portrayed in the works of Plato.

Plato's most famous work was *The Republic*. In it he tells the Allegory of the Cave, which takes us on a journey from existing in the darkness of ignorance to discovery and seeing the light. It has many meanings but we can think of it in the context of the importance of deep personal and social awareness and constant self-examination.

The Allegory of the Cave

Socrates, who is talking to Glaucon, the older brother of Plato, tells the allegory.

Socrates asks him to imagine a group which has been chained to the wall of a cave since childhood. They face a blank wall and cannot move their heads or legs. They watch shadows projected on the wall by other people who carry objects in front of a fire behind them. For the prisoners in the cave, the shadows of these objects have become reality.

Socrates: And now, I said, let me show in a figure how far our nature is enlightened or unenlightened: Behold! human beings living in an underground cave, which has a mouth open towards the light and reaching all along the cave; here they have been from their childhood, and have their legs and necks chained so that they cannot move, and can only see before them, being prevented by the chains from turning round their heads. Above and behind them a fire is blazing at a distance, and between the fire and the prisoners there is a raised way; and you will see, if you look, a low wall built along the way, like the screen which marionette players have in front of them, over which they show the puppets.

Glaucon: I see.

Socrates: And do you see, I said, men passing along the wall carrying all sorts of vessels, and statues and figures of animals made of wood and stone and various materials, which appear over the wall? Some of them are talking, others silent.

Glaucon says that it is a strange image, and that they are strange prisoners.

"Like ourselves" Socrates replies "they see only their own shadows, or the shadows of one another".

Socrates adds that if they were able to talk among themselves, they would assume that they were talking about what was actually in front of them. And that if the cave had an echo, they would think that when one of the passers-by spoke the voice they heard was actually coming from the passing shadow.

Glaucon agrees. Socrates continues by asking Glaucon to imagine what would happen if the prisoners were released from the cave after all those years.

At first able to stand, walk and look towards the light they would be in pain. The glare of light would distress them and they would be unable to see the realities of the situation. And if one of their former captors was to point at the objects they had previously only seen in shadow form as they pass, they would think that the shadows were truer than the objects they were now seeing.

Socrates suggests that if the freed prisoner was then dragged out of the cave into the presence of the sun his eyes would be dazzled. He would not be able to see anything at all of what are now called realities.

Glaucon agrees.

Socrates: He will need to grow accustomed to the sight of the upper world. And first he will see the shadows best, next the reflections of men and other objects in the water, and then the objects themselves; then he will gaze upon the light of the moon and the stars and the spangled heaven; and he will see the sky and the stars by night better than the sun or the light of the sun by day.

Glaucon: Certainly.

Socrates: Last of all he will be able to see the sun, and not mere reflections of him in the water, but he will see him in his own proper place, and not in another; and he will contemplate him as he is.

This was all over 2000 years ago. For us to be interesting as human beings it's probably a good idea to examine our lives and think about who we are and how we live.

Extracts of dialogue taken from the Benjamin Jowett translation of Plato's The Republic *(Vintage, 1991).*

1 KNOW YOURSELF

How to be interesting

Know yourself

If we're to look at what it means to be interesting and to begin to find out how interesting we might be as individuals, then we have to try to get to know ourselves. We need to gain some understanding of "what makes me, me". We need to look at what makes up our personality.

One of the most popular personality tools out there is called the Myers–Briggs Type Indicator or MBTI. It's said to be used by 89 of the Fortune 100 companies, and has been translated into 24 languages. Think of MBTI as a useful self-awareness tool rather than a test or in-depth psychological assessment.

Some people can be rather sceptical about this sort of thing, particularly when used in an employer–employee relationship, and correctly cite that there is no empirical evidence that the test results are accurate. But in our experience working out your Myers–Briggs profile can be illuminating, helpful and fun – just the process of self-examination alone is a useful trigger for you to think about where you are in life, how you can better understand yourself and how to interact with others. As an exercise, it certainly qualifies as interesting.

The MBTI aims to make Carl Gustav Jung's psychological types understandable to us in our everyday lives and, more importantly, useful. The typological theories were first proposed by Jung in his book *Psychological Types* in 1921.

Carl Gustav Jung

Swiss psychologist and psychiatrist Carl Jung (26 July 1875–6 June 1961) is credited as the founder of analytical psychology. Jung proposed and developed the concepts of the extroverted and the introverted personality.

He thought that the human psyche could be divided into three parts: the ego (the conscious and thinking self), the personal unconscious (collective personal experiences unique to each one of us) and the collective unconscious (the experiences and behaviour patterns that are common to everyone).

Psychological preferences

Mother and daughter team Katharine Briggs and Isabel Briggs Myers developed Jung's theories into The Myers–Briggs Type Indicator. It's a psychometric questionnaire that measures our psychological preferences in how we, as different individuals, perceive the world around us and how we make our decisions based on this perception.

To understand the MBTI we need to understand Jung's theory. He proposed that cognitive functions could be divided into two dichotomous pairs.

Cognitive function is all about knowing and processing thoughts. It includes aspects like awareness, perception, reasoning and judgement.

The two dichotomous pairs he proposed were:

1. The rational, judging functions of thinking and feeling.

2. The irrational, perceiving functions of sensing and intuition.

These, according to Jung, can be expressed in a further grouping of either introverted or extroverted form.

In this context by extroversion we mean "outward-turning" and by introversion we mean "inward-turning".

Jung thought of psychological type as somewhat like being left- or right-handed. Some of us write with our right hand, others with their left hand. Right-handed people can write with their left hand (if they have to) but prefer to use their right hand.

Jung said that in a similar way individuals were born with, or developed over time, preferred ways of thinking and acting.

The MBTI groups these differences into four opposite pairs or dichotomies, which results in 16 possible psychological types. It is important to note that none of these types are better than others – it's just that individuals have natural preferences.

The four dichotomies

The four opposite pairs are known by their initial letters except for intuition, which is known as N, as in iNtuition. So the four pairs are:

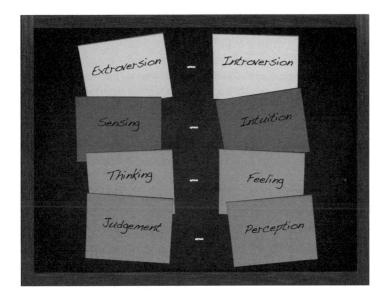

Extroversion–Introversion

These preferences are sometimes called attitudes. Here, extroversion means "outward-turning" and introversion means "inward-turning". An extrovert type personality is directed out towards people and objects while an introvert type personality is directed inward toward concepts and ideas.

People with a preference for extroversion tend to act first, then reflect, then act further. They are often considered good talkers.

People with a preference for introversion tend to reflect carefully first, then act, then reflect again. They are often considered good listeners.

Sensing–Intuition

These are the two perceiving or information-gathering functions.

People who prefer sensing are more likely to trust information that is tangible and solid. They are often interested in small detail and facts. They prefer to trust experience and reality.

People who prefer intuition tend to trust information that is more abstract or theoretical. They tend to focus on the big picture and often prefer to trust their instincts.

Thinking–Feeling

These are the two judging or decision-making functions.

They are used to make rational decisions, based on the information received from their sensing or intuition functions.

People who prefer thinking often tend to decide things from a detached view based on logic and reason. They are often goal focused and make decisions with their head.

People who prefer feeling often reach decisions by associating or empathizing with the situation. They are often subjective in their decision-making, like to maintain harmony and make decisions with their heart.

Judgement–Perception

People also have a preference for how they use their judging function and their perceiving function in relation to the outside world.

People who prefer judging are often planned and organized in their daily routines. They are often task driven and don't like last minute changes or surprises.

People who prefer perceiving can appear to have no plan of action. They are often flexible, adaptable and enjoy acting on spontaneity. They thrive on variety.

16 possible psychological types

The 16 possible psychological types are referred to as abbreviations of four letters. There are plenty of websites that list the MBTI types of famous people, some of which we've shown here – though how accurate these are is anyone's guess of course!

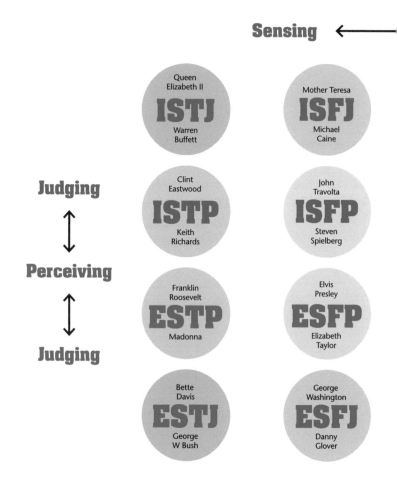

⟶ Intuitive

Nelson Mandela

ISFJ

Nicole
Kidman

Dwight
D. Eisenhower

INTJ

Martina
Navratilova

Audrey
Hepburn

INFP

JRR
Tolkien

Albert
Einstein

INTP

Marie
Curie

Introvert

↕

Extrovert

Sandra
Bullock

ENFP

Robin
Williams

Walt Disney

ENTP

Tom Hanks

Johnny
Depp

ENFJ

Kirstie
Alley

Bill
Gates

ENTJ

Sigourney
Weaver

⟶ Thinking

The MBTI questionnaire looks at how a person perceives the world and how they prefer to interact with others. It helps people improve their working and personal relationships in a positive and constructive way by helping them understand their personality in more depth. It helps you to:

- Understand your own and others' behaviours in greater depth.
- Approach problems in different yet healthy ways.
- Understand and utilize your natural strengths.
- Improve teamwork.
- Resolve conflict.

It can be really useful when it comes to extracting more value from your personal and working relationships. It may feel like problems all arise out of other people's shortcomings, but you'd be amazed how much easier life is when you're aware of your own strengths and weaknesses. Myers–Briggs can help you understand your own personality in more depth, and this, in turn, impacts upon the way you deal with others. Don't knock it till you've tried it. Who knows, you might find it interesting.

An ISTJ – Introvert, Sensing, Thinking and Judging type personality, like Warren Buffett, is no better or worse than an ENTJ – Extrovert, Intuitive, Thinking and Judging type personality such as Margaret Thatcher. They are simply different personality types.

Likewise, someone who prefers judgement to perception is not, by definition, more judgmental or less perceptive.

And someone who scores high for extroversion as opposed to introversion is not a more extroverted person necessarily. They just have a clearer preference for extroversion.

To take the MBTI personality type indicator

The MBTI takes the form of a simple questionnaire of forced-choice questions where the individual has to choose one of two possible answers to each question. The choices are a combination of word pairs and short statements. Choices are not literal opposites, rather they aim to reflect the opposite preferences on the same dichotomy.

There are 88 questions in the European English version and 93 in the North American English version.

We are the best judges of our own type

In MBTI individuals are thought to be the best judge of their own type. The questionnaire gives a *Reported Type* but this is only an indication of the probable *Overall Type*. During feedback, a *Best-Fit* discussion helps the individual increase their understanding of the four dichotomies and decide on the personality type closest to their own.

Considered feedback is important

It's best when taking the assessment to get detailed feedback from a trained MBTI practitioner with a Best-Fit exercise and discussion to check against the Reported Type.

Type not trait

The MBTI sorts only for personality preferences – it's not about assessing strength of ability.

No right or wrong

No preference or total type is better or worse than another – all are equal.

Not for selection

Because MBTI measures preferences not aptitude, it should not be used for employment selection.

> The original Latin meaning of the word character is an inscription or marking that differentiates one thing from another for identification purposes. In ancient Greek "charaktér" is an engraving

What's my type?

Here are a few examples of the sort of questions that are asked in the MBTI questionnaire. These are not actual questions from the MBTI; they are merely to give you an idea of the type of questions asked.

You prefer to plan ahead rather than do things on the spur of the moment
☐ Yes ☐ No

You are more interested in general ideas than in the specific details
☐ Yes ☐ No

You trust reason above personal feelings
☐ Yes ☐ No

You like helping people, expecting nothing in return
☐ Yes ☐ No

You easily sympathize with other people
☐ Yes ☐ No

You often prefer to read a novel than go to a party
☐ Yes ☐ No

You enjoy putting things in order
☐ Yes ☐ No

You feel comfortable and at ease in a crowd
☐ Yes ☐ No

You often make decisions based on the feelings of the moment rather than on careful planning
☐ Yes ☐ No

You like to keep your desk or workspace neat and ordered
☐ Yes ☐ No

You find talking about your feelings difficult
☐ Yes ☐ No

What personality type do you think you might be? ❓

Knowing me,

Knowing you,

Aha

Abba and Alan Partridge
(or maybe it should be the other way around).

Holding the interest of others

If you are attuned to the way a person is feeling, you are more likely to hold their interest than someone who is not receptive to what is happening beneath the surface. Developing your emotional intelligence is one way of helping to improve your understanding of others and your relationships.

What is emotional intelligence?

Emotional intelligence is sometimes known as EQ or EI. It's all about the ability to perceive, control and evaluate our emotions. It's about self-awareness and self-motivation.

Emotional intelligence theory was first developed by psychologists Gardner, Salovey and Mayer in the 1970s and 1980s. Daniel Goleman further developed the concept in his book *Emotional Intelligence* (1995).

Salovey and Mayer defined emotional intelligence as, "the subset of social intelligence that involves the ability to monitor one's own and others' feelings and emotions, to discriminate among them and to use this information to guide one's thinking and actions".

In Daniel Goleman's book – *Emotional Intelligence* – he says that EI creates social abilities that: "… allow one to shape an encounter, to mobilise and inspire others, to thrive in intimate relationships, to persuade and influence, to put others at ease".

Goleman identified five "domains" of emotional intelligence:

1. Knowing your emotions.
2. Managing your own emotions.
3. Motivating yourself.
4. Recognizing and understanding other people's emotions.
5. Managing relationships; that is, managing the emotions of others.

The subtitle to the book is: "Why it Can Matter More than IQ".

He goes on to say:

> "People with well-developed emotional skills are more likely to be content and effective in their lives, mastering the habits of mind that foster their own productivity."

Goleman's poser of "Why it Can Matter More than IQ" is a very interesting one. We are sometimes drawn to people with high intellects because they often have interesting things to say – and that's great.

But if a person has a high IQ and is able to match it with a high EQ – even better?

Truly great leaders have a high EQ. They know what inspires and motivates. They know how to make people feel good about themselves. They hear the unheard. They understand the value of emotional investment. They are interesting people.

People with high emotional intelligence are good at understanding other people's feelings and managing relationships.

Because high emotional intelligence helps us interact better with people, it plays a very important role in being interesting.

It is worth noting that a high IQ does not necessarily translate to having a high EQ or EI.

How high is your EQ? However high it is, it could probably be higher. Take every opportunity to work on this facet of your character. There's always room for improvement! Do one thing this week to start growing this part of your identity. Next time you're talking to a friend, listen harder ...

Brain power

We can't really look at the whole subject of being interesting and how humans think and behave without talking briefly about the human brain.

Our brain performs an incredible number of tasks.

- It controls body temperature, blood pressure, heart rate and breathing.
- It takes in and processes masses of information about the world around us. This information is fed in from our senses of seeing, hearing, smelling, tasting and touching.
- It manages the physical movement of our body.
- It enables us to think, reason, dream and experience emotions.

Left-brain–right-brain theory

According to the theory of left-brain or right-brain dominance, each side of the brain controls different types of thinking. It is thought that people prefer one type of thinking to the other.

Someone who is "left-brained" is often said to be more logical, analytical and objective.

Someone who is "right-brained" is often thought to be more intuitive, thoughtful and subjective.

This theory is based on something called the lateralization of brain function. But is it true that one side of the brain controls specific functions? Are people really either left-brained or right-brained?

The right-brain–left-brain theory stemmed from the work of Roger Sperry, who won the Nobel Prize in 1981.

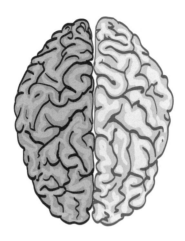

Language – Logic	Recognizing faces – Expressing emotions
Analytical thinking	Music – Reading emotions
Critical thinking – Numbers – Reasoning	Colour – Images
	Intuition – Creativity

Are you more a right-side or left-side of the brain thinker?

We use both sides of the brain but tend to use one more than the other.

But are you more of a right-side or left-side of the brain thinker?

Try one of the many left-brain, right-brain tests on the web and make your own mind up about how indicative they are.

There's also the spinning dancer test (Google it, you'll find it easily).

Which way do you see her spinning? Clockwise or anti-clockwise?

According to some, if you see her spinning anti-clockwise you're more left-brained. If you see her spinning clockwise you're more right-brained.

According to others, it's just a clever optical illusion (it's the latter btw.)

Some interesting things about the human brain

☺ The average adult brain weighs about 3 lbs – between 1300 and 1400 grams.

☺ There's an iPad app that gives you a detailed view of Einstein's brain. It was removed without permission at his autopsy and preserved.

☺ The brain is made up of about 75% water. Although about 2% of body weight it uses about 20% of the oxygen in our blood.

☺ The brain's grey matter is made up of neurons, which gather and transmit signals. The white matter is made up of dendrites and axons, which create the network by which neurons send their signals. The brain is 60% white matter and 40% grey matter.

☺ There are anywhere from 1000 to 10 000 synapses for each neuron.

☺ It is believed that humans experience, on average, 70 000 thoughts each day.

☺ It is a myth that you only use 10% of your brain – every part of the brain has a function.

☺ It pays to keep exercising your brain, because mental activity stimulates the creation of new neurons throughout your whole life.

☺ While you are asleep you are practically paralyzed as your brain creates a hormone to stop you acting out your dreams.

☺ About 12% of us dream in black and white.

☺ There are 100 000 miles of blood vessels in the brain.

☺ The brain has no pain receptors so it cannot feel pain. Sorry Monty Python but there is no such thing as "my brain hurts".

A reminder

As we have said, this is not an instructional manual. So, unlike some instructional personal development books, we have avoided the use of irritating or silly mnemonics.

You know the sort of thing we mean?

Plan, Review, Action, Target

Remember it as

PRAT

But while we're here …

Even though we think mnemonic devices are a bit silly, it's worth mentioning that they may well help us be interesting. Why? Because they are learning techniques that help us remember information and information makes people interesting.

Mnemonics translate information into a form that the brain finds easier to retain and recall. It is suggested that the actual process of converting a word or phrase into a mnemonic may help the transfer of information to long-term memory.

Back in the times of the Ancient Greeks and Romans differences were distinguished between two types of memory: the "natural" memory and the "artificial" memory. The first is inborn – the one we use automatically – the second is trained and developed through learning.

So do mnemonics actually work? Well, Mark's grandmother, god rest her soul, was very big on mnemonics. She taught him three when he was a small child.

Richard Of York Gave Battle In Vain – for the colours of the rainbow Red, Orange, Yellow, Green, Blue, Indigo, Violet.

Never Eat Cake Eat Salmon Sandwiches And Remain Young – for the word Necessary.

Big Elephants Can Always Understand Small Elephants – for the word Because.

He has always remembered all of them. He was never taught "A friend is always there when the end comes". Which is maybe why he still spells the word friend incorrectly sometimes.

There's even a mnemonic for mnemonic apparently:

Mnemonics Now Erase Man's Oldest Nemesis, Insufficient Cerebral Storage.

So people use mnemonics because the human mind can remember spatial, personal information more easily than it remembers rather abstract, impersonal information. Putting it in a personal context seems to lodge it into our brain.

With that in mind, we would like to employ at least one mnemonic device in this book. You'll find it over the page.

TANAMITB

There are no annoying mnemonics in this book.

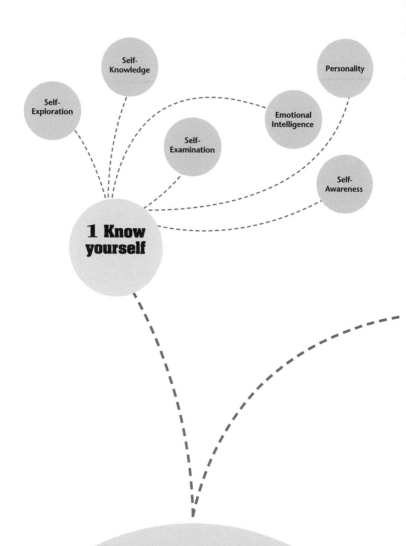

Self-Exploration

Self-Knowledge

Personality

Self-Examination

Emotional Intelligence

Self-Awareness

1 Know yourself

How to be interesting

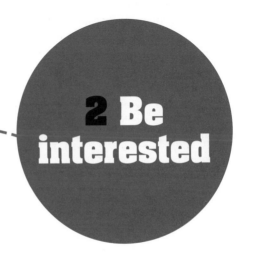

**2 Be
interested**

Interested in everything around you = being interesting

In *Hitch-22*, Christopher Hitchens's marvellous memoirs, he writes in the acknowledgements section that his "promiscuous mandate is to be interested in everything".

Who was Christopher Hitchens? A marvellous polymath who managed to make a life out of disagreeing with almost everyone in a way that made them only love him more. His unpredictability, contrariness, and biting wit might have made him enemies, but instead his rampant enthusiasm for life ensured that when he died in 2011 he did so with friends from almost every walk of life. His funeral was a celebration of his interest in things and ideas.

It isn't just brilliant writers like Hitchens who should try to be interested in everything. We should all be interested in everything around us. It's this interest, after all, that makes us interesting.

"Under pressure, people admit to murder, setting fire to the village church or robbing a bank, but never to being bores."

Elsa Maxwell, columnist and party hostess who was dubbed "The Hostess with the Mostest" by the press in the mid-20th century

Do I have to be interested to be interesting?

❝ *When I was at drama school I shared a flat with some of my fellow students. One of them I found particularly interesting. He was a Canadian called Jim Walker. Jim was, and no doubt still is, an extremely intelligent man with a photographic memory which made him the envy of all of us when it came to learning lines. He also had an insatiable appetite for knowledge. We only shared the flat for one term but in that short period of time Jim had taught himself to speak Norwegian – the reason being there were two students from Norway in his year so he felt it the right thing to do. He also taught himself to play the banjo to a very high standard and was well on his way to becoming a gourmet cook! This was all relaxation to Jim but if he really wanted to switch off and chill out, he would find a comfy chair in a quiet corner and do a few pure maths problems! He was also a fine actor and what probably helped him in his development as an actor was the wealth of knowledge he had of the world around him and the people in it. But the really interesting thing about Jim was his genuine interest in us.* **❞**

- Dave

Do I have to be interested to be interesting?

An interest in others is particularly prevalent in face-to-face interaction. We alluded to this briefly in our boring section. We cannot help but enjoy the attention and interest of other people. So, on that basis, does showing an interest in others help create or keep their interest in us?

It is very flattering to have an interest shown in us. It makes us feel important, respected, valued and worthwhile. The reason we feel that way is because the interest is pushing our emotional feel good buttons. If we are able to do this to others it becomes easier to get their attention and hopefully gain their interest.

There is a possibility, of course, that we might be conning their subconscious into being interested in us, but does it matter?

There is the wonderful story about the woman who had dinner with William Gladstone one evening and Benjamin Disraeli the next evening. She said:

> "After having dinner with Mr Gladstone I felt that he was the most intelligent man in the country. After having dinner with Mr Disraeli I felt that I was the most intelligent woman in the country."

Showing interest in people makes them feel good about themselves.

Would you rather be a Gladstone or a Disraeli?

Are you Interesting or Interesting?

Life is short, make the most of every moment

An atmosphere of interest

So what is in the ether when there is an interaction between two or more people who are feeling interested and/or interesting?

For this, we turn to Dr Tara Swart for a neuroscience insight on how to be interesting.

On a deep, primitive level of instinct, within the emotional centres of the brain, we can sense if another person is interested in us and this is more likely to make us interested in them.

To come across as genuinely interested, a socially appropriate level of eye contact and a style and level of listening that is about attempting to understand the other person, rather than interjecting with a clever question or even an anecdote of your own on the topic, are the key foundations. When two people do this, an emotional resonance loop develops between your brains on several levels:

Neurochemically, your brain starts to release dopamine in the reward areas of the brain – this neurochemical is associated with getting something you want; opiods are released when you get something you like; serotonin release is associated with being in a good mood. Oxytocin is in the air when trust is growing and when you are falling in love! It is a hormone secreted by the hypothalamus which induces a calm, warm mood that increases tender feelings and attachment, and may lead us to lower our guard. This is perhaps the hormone most fundamental to being interesting; noradrenaline intensifies the effects of all of the above and is involved in attention and concentration; cortisol (stress) levels should be low in this scenario.

Feelings are combinations of the eight basic sets of human emotions (fear, anger, disgust, shame, sadness, surprise/startle, joy/excitement, love/trust).

Evidence from research into inter-personal neurobiology would suggest that being interested is to feel curiosity about, or a desire to know, and is a manifestation of the surprise/startle emotion combined with excitement and trust.

The brain is all about inter-connectedness – our genetic make-up combined with all our life experiences, from the womb, parenting styles, learning preferences, talent choices, social milieu, gender, culture, relationships and many, many more factors, create a unique blueprint of who we are, what we find interesting and who and what we attract into our lives, which continues to shape us into the future.

In a nutshell, being interesting would appear to involve being aware of and able to regulate the impact of our brain on that of another. It is about providing enough, but not too much, novelty, challenge and choice to engage and motivate. Neuroplasticity – the ability of the brain to learn, unlearn and relearn – means that we can develop skills even if they are not already a strong part of our toolkit. We can learn explicitly by something like reading this book, as well as implicitly through the lessons we pick up in life. Look out for someone interesting and ponder what you can learn from them.

My oxytocin levels have gone crazy!

An interesting aside on the subject of phrenology

Phrenology was developed from the work of the German physician Franz Joseph Gall around 1800. Noticing that the cerebral cortex of humans was much larger than that of animals, he came to believe that it was this that made humans intellectually superior.

He went on to propose the theory that the physical features of the cortex could also be seen in the shape and size of the skull.

His theory went something like this:

The brain is the organ of the mind.

The mind is made up of multiple distinct, innate faculties.

As they are distinct, each faculty must have a separate place or "organ" in the brain.

The size of an organ is related to its power.

The shape of the brain is determined by the development of the various organs.

As the skull takes its shape from the brain, the surface of the skull can be read as an accurate measure of psychological traits.

Gall went on to measure the skulls of people that he found in prisons, hospitals, and other institutions. Then, based on his results, he designed a system of 27 different "faculties" that he believed could be linked to parts of the head.

He designed a chart to show which parts of the skull were associated with each particular characteristic.

The 27 different skull "faculties" of phrenology are shown here in all their bonkers glory

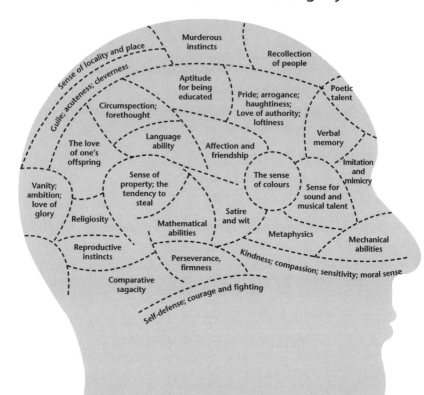

Murderous instincts

Recollection of people

Sense of locality and place

Guile; acuteness; cleverness

Aptitude for being educated

Pride; arrogance; haughtiness; Love of authority; loftiness

Poetic talent

Circumspection; forethought

Verbal memory

Language ability

Affection and friendship

The love of one's offspring

Imitation and mimicry

Vanity; ambition; love of glory

Sense of property; the tendency to steal

The sense of colours

Sense for sound and musical talent

Religiosity

Satire and wit

Mathematical abilities

Metaphysics

Mechanical abilities

Reproductive instincts

Perseverance, firmness

Kindness; compassion; sensitivity; moral sense

Comparative sagacity

Self-defense; courage and fighting

People found it so interesting that they believed it!

Phrenology became so popular that by 1832 there were 29 phrenological societies in London alone.

In the 1820s–1840s it was not uncommon for employers to ask for a character reference from a local phrenologist to check that a potential employee was hard-working and trustworthy.

Sanity eventually prevailed; phrenology's popularity faded and it eventually became viewed in the same light as astrology, numerology and palmistry.

Some of the "faculties" of being interesting?

Thirst for knowledge

Empathy   Emotional intelligence

Embrace change   Be positive   Confidence

Self-awareness   Be optimistic

Be generous – share your thoughts and experiences

Ask questions   Personality   Listen properly

Compassion   Be cheerful   Use of language

Love learning   Innovation   Manners

Be interested in others and in everything

Sense of humour   Self-knowledge   Be creative

MBTI   Performance   Respect for others

Presence   Be open, warm and accessible

Be active – do things   Hobbies and interests

Self-examination   Happy in yourself

Be curious and inquisitive   Self-esteem

Good work/life balance

Love music, arts, culture, science   Develop passions

Tell stories

Why learning *How to be Interesting* is a bit like learning *How to Win Friends and Influence People*

How to Win Friends and Influence People was one of the first best-selling self-help books published. It was written by Dale Carnegie and first published in 1936. Since then it has sold more than 15 million copies across the world.

We recommend it without hesitation.

If you've never read it we suggest that you read it as soon as you've finished this little book.

If you've read it before, read it again to remind you.

Naturally, it will help you learn how to win friends and how to influence people. But it will also help you learn how to be interesting. The three factors are closely related.

Here are just two of the many wise things that Carnegie said about his philosophy that still resonate with us today.

The first always makes us smile:

> "When fate hands you a lemon, make lemonade."

And the second always makes us think:

> "Remember, happiness doesn't depend upon who you are or what you have; it depends solely on what you think."

One of his big central ideas is that you can change other people's behaviour by changing your reaction to them.

The following section was in the original 1936 edition as a single page list. We thought it'd be interesting to show this to you – as, with the probable exception of earning power, notice how we can relate all of these things to *How to be Interesting*:

Twelve Things This Book Will Do For You

- Get you out of a mental rut; give you new thoughts, new visions, new ambitions.
- Enable you to make friends quickly and easily.
- Increase your popularity.
- Help you to win people to your way of thinking.
- Increase your influence, your prestige, your ability to get things done.
- Enable you to win new clients, new customers.
- Increase your earning power.
- Make you a better salesman, a better executive.
- Help you to handle complaints, avoid arguments, keep your human contacts smooth and pleasant.
- Make you a better speaker, a more entertaining conversationalist.
- Make the principles of psychology easy for you to apply in your daily contacts.
- Help you to arouse enthusiasm among your associates.

Likewise, this section about how to make people like you could easily be rephrased as how to get people to find you interesting:

Six Ways to Make People Like You

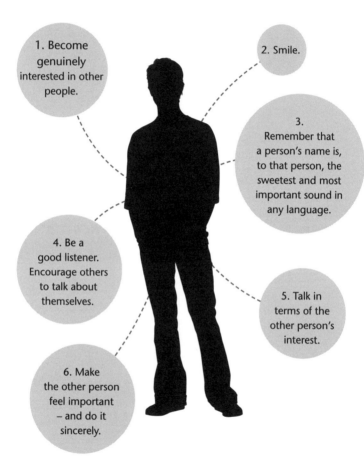

1. Become genuinely interested in other people.

2. Smile.

3. Remember that a person's name is, to that person, the sweetest and most important sound in any language.

4. Be a good listener. Encourage others to talk about themselves.

5. Talk in terms of the other person's interest.

6. Make the other person feel important – and do it sincerely.

Finally, notice how the points in this section from Carnegie's book are directly relevant to *How to be Interesting*:

Twelve Ways to Win People to Your Way of Thinking

1. The only way to get the best of an argument is to avoid it.
2. Show respect for the other person's opinions. Never say "You're wrong".
3. If you're wrong, admit it quickly and emphatically.
4. Begin in a friendly way.
5. Start with questions to which the other person will answer yes.
6. Let the other person do a great deal of the talking.
7. Let the other person feel the idea is his or hers.
8. Try honestly to see things from the other person's point of view.
9. Be sympathetic with the other person's ideas and desires.
10. Appeal to the nobler motives.
11. Dramatize your ideas.
12. Throw down a challenge.

Carnegie was proud that he developed his views from a host of other sources. As he said, "The ideas I stand for are not mine. I borrowed them from Socrates. I swiped them from Chesterfield. I stole them from Jesus. And I put them in a book. If you don't like their rules whose would you use?"

Carnegie had wanted to act and trained at the American Academy of Dramatic Arts in New York but he didn't succeed as an actor. His middle name was Breckenridge.

Ever noticed that you hardly ever buy from someone you don't like?

Anyone experienced in sales will maintain that it is the salesperson who must first sell himself or herself before they can sell the product.

Good salespeople take a healthy interest in their customers. They do not look at them as their next conquest. They become interested in them as individuals and want advice to help them make the right decisions.

Good selling has two simple stages. Stage one means taking sufficient interest in the customer to find out what their needs and requirements are and then assuring the customer that they are able to cater for them. This is personal stuff. This is taking interest in order to guide and steer. This is getting rid of the salesperson tag and becoming a trusted advisor.

Stage two is making sure that the trusted advice has been taken on board and the decision is to buy the product. When this process works well it is because a good salesperson has made sure that both sides are interested in each other.

66 Before I went off to college I was a travelling salesman like my father. One day I asked Dad for some tips on being better at the job. He gave me one piece of advice. He told me to buy a huge diary – A4, if not bigger, with a page a day. He then told me to write as much as I could remember about the conversation I had with the customer after the call, particularly birthdays, weddings, ailments, holidays etc. – personal things. The next time I called on them, my Dad promised me that if I could engage them with just one piece of personal information they had shared with me before – I would get the order. Dad is now in his early 80s but still visits his old customers because through their mutual trust and interest they have made the transition from clients to friends. 99

- *Dave*

66 Both our fathers were salesmen at some stage in their careers. My Dad too gave me some advice. It was when I was still at primary school. I remember him explaining very carefully to me that whenever I met someone I should look them in the eyes, smile and shake their hand firmly and warmly. I remember at the time thinking "It's not that important is it, Dad? All you're talking about is saying hello!" But looking back it was probably some of the best advice I was ever given. 99

- *Mark*

It's just as important to be interested in others as it is to be interesting

Here's Doctor Tim Anstis on how to be interesting and being interested. Tim trained in occupational medicine and is an expert in CBT – Cognitive Behaviour Therapy – and Motivational Interviewing.

If you want to develop good, healthy relationships with other human beings, you need to be genuinely interested – not just faking interest to advance your personal agenda. As the philosopher Kant said, we should treat the person as an end in themselves, and not just a means to an end.

These are the basic building blocks on which to show real, genuine interest.

1. Open questions

Open questions are questions that are hard to answer with just one word. They encourage the other person to talk, to describe, to elaborate, to explore and to continue talking. Examples of open questions include:

- *Then what happened?*
- *Why do you think she did that?*
- *How did you feel?*
- *So, what's next for you?*

Now obviously you don't want to be just using open questions. That would make the conversation feel like a bit of an interrogation. But they are really helpful in moving the conversation along and helping the person feel that they are interesting and that you are interested in them.

2. Affirmations

Affirmations are statements that recognize something good about the person – perhaps the effort they have put in, their attitude, a skill or a strength you have spotted. They go deeper to the core of a person than "your hair looks lovely" or "nice car". They sound like this:

- *You really know how to bring the best out in others.*
- *That was a brave thing to do.*
- *You're making a real effort.*
- *You have a real passion for this kind of work.*

Again, your conversation should not just be one long stream of affirmations. Firstly, you can't do this since you need to use the raw material the person provides in the conversation in order to make the affirmation. And secondly, it would make the conversation awkward and the listener suspicious. So throw them in every now and again. Just one or two. Use them like seasoning. Lightly and skillfully.

3. Reflections

Reflections involve you saying back to the person something of what they said, but not in the same words they used. They help the person to "hear" what they have said, feel that you are making the effort to understand them, and can sometimes lead to them understanding themselves better. You can make simple, complex and double-sided reflections.

Simple reflections might sound like this:

They say ...	You say ...
"Why did they do that?"	*"It's hard for you to understand"*
"I'm not sure what to do right now"	*"You've got some more thinking to do"*

| "I'm so excited" | "You're really looking forward to this" |

Human beings have a very strong inner drive to be understood, not misunderstood. Use this to your advantage.

Double-sided reflections might sound like this (depending on what the person has just said)

- "You want to lose weight, but you can't see yourself taking more exercise"
- "Part of you wants to stay with him, and you're also worried you might be missing out"
- "You see the advantages of doing the course, but then you wouldn't be able to take this trip"
- "Placing a deposit will help you get on the housing market, which is important, and you are also a bit worried about whether or not you can keep up the repayments"

You can use a "but" or an "and" to make the contrast. Using "but" comes easier to me, but tends to be dismissive of what was said before. I am trying to use more "ands" in my double-sided reflections.

4. Summaries

Summaries are longer reflections, bringing together several elements of what the other person has said – both to check you have understood them correctly, to help them to hear what they have just said, and in preparation for perhaps moving the conversation off in another direction or bringing it to a close. You might ask permission before you summarize. A summary might sound something like this:

"Can I just check I am understanding all this correctly? So, you've been doing this job for three months now, and...."

Done well and at the right time, summaries can be really powerful in helping the other person feel heard and understood. Like affirmations, use them sparingly.

Another tip for strengthening your relationship with others: be curious when they bring you good news. Get them to talk about it more, to explain and explore it. This typically brings forward good feelings in both parties.

Let's say you meet a friend who you haven't seen for a while and they tell you they have just been promoted. You could say something like:

"Really? So, what shall we do later?" [ignoring what they said]

Or you could say:

"Really? My job is shit at the moment. I really feel stuck in a rut." [talking about yourself]

Or you could say:

"Oh yeah? Won't that be more stress? And the travel, that's an extra hour each day/You must be mad." [being negative about their news]

Or you could say:

"Wow. How are you feeling? (then listen). What are you looking forward to most? (then listen). Why do you think they chose you?" etc.

The latter is called active-constructive responding and is something we can all get better at.

It shows that we are genuinely interested and so makes us interesting.

Arne L. Schmidt is a Hollywood producer and writer. His movie credits include blockbusters like *Robocop* and he's worked with a host of stars. Through his work, he has recognized the impact of taking an interest in others.

66 *I remember sitting on set with one of the actors waiting for the lighting to be ready. We were only a few days into filming, so this was a first chance to get to know him. I thought I could "make myself interesting" by asking him a little about himself, thinking he would almost certainly like the subject matter. I asked him how he got into the business. I thought it was a harmless question, but I was very wrong. It hadn't occurred to me that my question was exactly like the boring questions he had to endure while doing publicity for his last movie. I pulled back and regrouped.*

His birthday was coming up and I went to a bookstore looking for something that he might enjoy. He had told me he was planning a trip around the world on a motorcycle when the movie was over and I discovered a book written by someone who had done just that. At his birthday party, when I gave him the book, he lit up. Here was something he and I were both passionate about, motorcycling, and we had a lively and lengthy conversation about riding. I had numerous different bikes throughout my life so I could speak with knowledge and enthusiasm about them. That was a big lesson for me in the art of being interesting. 99

Be generous

Interesting people are generous
of spirit and mind.

"Treat others how you would like to be treated"

This is the Golden Rule that can be found in some form in almost every ethical tradition. It's a very strong foundation of ethical thinking but can be forgotten all too quickly.

Jesus preached, "So in everything, do unto others as you would have them do unto you...."

Confucius taught "What you do not wish for yourself, do not do to others ... as you help yourself desire standing, then help others achieve it; as you yourself desire success, then help others attain it." And Muhammad said, "Hurt no one so that no one may hurt you."

To be interesting it's important to treat others as you would like to be treated. To be interesting we have to be interested in others. That means showing them respect.

In 1963 when US President John F Kennedy spoke out against race discrimination and race segregation, he used the Golden Rule very eloquently to make his point and get his audience interested: "The heart of the question is whether all Americans are to be afforded equal rights and equal opportunities, whether we are going to treat our fellow Americans as we want to be treated."

This Golden Rule is universal in its appeal.

If to be interesting is to be interested, then surely we should use it all the time?

Philosophically, it is about us perceiving other people as "an I", "me" or "self" as well.

Psychologically, it's about us empathizing with others.

> **Do you follow the Golden Rule?** Most of us try to, but it's easy to fall short. Try to ask yourself this question when you're interacting with other people; you'll soon find that applying the rule becomes more and more natural.

Empathy

There are many different definitions of the word empathy.

It can mean caring for other people and wanting to help them.

It can mean experiencing emotions that match the emotions of another person.

It can mean being able to relate to the feelings, thoughts or attitudes of others.

It can mean to know what another person is thinking or feeling,

Empathy helps us understand and anticipate the behaviour of those around us.

To be interesting we need empathy.

The British psychologist, Edward Titchener, first introduced the term "empathy" into the English language in 1909. It is a translation of the German "Einfühlung" – "feeling into".

Open or closed? What's the more welcoming?

"I'm a very open-minded person." We've all said it but do we mean it? No, do we really mean it? "I'm as open-minded as the next person." Yes – but who is the next person? Is it one of those things we say when we have actually closed our minds off to anything other than the opinion we have already decided to take?

Wouldn't it be great to have an open mind? Imagine that! Letting everything in. Oh, the joy of sifting through all that glorious information! Most of us don't and possibly never will – but should that stop us trying to be genuinely open-minded?

An open mind has got to be a wonderful thing. To be able to form opinion without prejudice would take a very interesting person.

Someone capable of listening, processing information with clear and untainted thinking and responding with unfettered feeling would be a very interesting person indeed.

Are you listening?

The outside of the ear is shaped like a question mark – for a very good reason.

The better a communicator someone is, the more interesting they are likely to be. And one of the secrets of being a great communicator is a very simple skill.

Everyone can learn this skill but a lot of people never bother for some reason. It's not that they don't want to be able to do it. It's more that they're unaware of its power.

This skill? It's called listening. Yes, that's right, that thing we do with our ears … and our brains.

Learn to listen – to really listen – and you are immediately interesting to other people because you're showing them that you're interested in them.

Now there's listening and really listening. Let's take a quick look at some of the many different types of listening.

Biased listening

This is when the person only hears what they want to hear. They very typically misinterpret what the other person says based on biased opinions that they already have.

Arrogant listening

We've all had this done to us and some of us may have been guilty of it ourselves. This is the sort of listener who responds to what has been said to them with a "I knew that already and knew more than you anyway" attitude. They aren't listening, they are point scoring.

Selective listening

This is listening for particular things and ignoring anything else. They hear only what they want to hear and pay little or no attention to anything else.

Distracted listening

Distracted, or detached, listening is when the person listening isn't 100% there. They are disengaged from what you say and are irritatingly distracted by anything other than what you are saying to them. It sends out the clear signal that they are not interested in you at all. They would rather either be somewhere else or talking to someone other than you. Not pleasant.

Interrupted listening

Interrupted listening is when the listener (sic) really wants to talk about another subject and is always on the lookout for opportunities to interrupt and change the direction of the conversation.

Even more insulting, they often have decided for you (because they are sooo clever) how your thought and sentence should end. So they do you the favour of ending your sentence for you. Thanks a bunch.

Aggressive listening

This is very annoying. The aggressive listener, so determined to demonstrate to you that they are listening, uses excessive body language and facial expressions that are meant to send out the message I AM LISTENING.

The trouble is they are not hearing a word you utter. They make you want to scream, "Rather than keep doing this with your hands and nod to show me you're listening – just sit still, look me in the eye and listen properly".

There's also another variant of this: the argumentative listener. They listen only because they want to disagree with whatever you say.

Partial listening

This is the type of listening that the majority of people often engage in. We listen to the other person with the best of intentions but then get distracted. The distraction can be caused by internal random stray thoughts or by something that the other person has said. By the time we rejoin the conversation and start listening properly, we've probably lost the thread.

Full listening

This is when the listener pays very close and careful attention to what is being said. They also try very carefully to understand the speaker and what they are trying to put across.

By the end of the conversation, the listener and the speaker should be able to agree that the listener understands well what was said.

Full listening requires concentration and skills of understanding.

Active listening

This is real listening. It is effective listening. It builds rapport, understanding and trust. The following six things help us to become an active listener.

1. Treat the other person how you would like to be treated.
2. Give them your complete and undivided attention.
3. Listen to every word.
4. Show that you're listening with the appropriate verbal and non-verbal responses. (Not bad acting of the "this-is-fascinating" type.)
5. Give your carefully considered feedback with honesty.
6. Show that you both understand and respect their opinions.

By taking a genuine interest in what another person has to say to us and allowing our comments to flow as a natural result of what we are hearing, we will be listening actively.

It shows we care about "who" the person is and "what they have to say". It shows that we respect them and find what they have to say interesting.

I love Brad – he's such an active listener.

Try to listen as actively as possible and steer clear of the other types of listening.

Giving someone your undivided attention
= being interested in them
= being interesting

A simple equation anyone can use, but many don't.

Not listening to someone is just as bad as ignoring them – and everyone hates to be ignored. We don't find people who ignore us interesting do we? We find them annoying, ignorant or rude.

We don't want to know more about people who ignore us.

We are not attracted to or drawn to people who ignore us. We feel pushed away or more likely we walk away. It's the same with listening. Listen well and often. It makes us interesting.

Listening is a skill that everyone can get better at. It's also something where it's all too easy to slip back into bad habits. Hands up anyone who's ever interrupted someone while they've been talking to you. We thought so, pretty much everybody – including ourselves.

Work at becoming a better listener: it improves your ability to influence and persuade. It also makes you more interesting.

Remember, interesting people are interested in other people and their stories.

To put it another way, as Mia Wallace (Uma Thurman) said to Vincent Vega (John Travolta) in Quentin Tarantino's *Pulp Fiction* when she met him for the first time,

   "Do you listen or do you wait to talk?"

"If you can't say something nice, don't say nothing at all"

The young rabbit Thumper in the film *Bambi* as he repeats his father's advice.

INT.STUDY.DAY

Dave and Mark review progress.

                    MARK

Whenever I look at the section on types of
listening, I feel a bit guilty.

                    DAVE

Why?

                    MARK

Because I don't listen to people really properly
all the time.

                    DAVE

Not unusual.

                    MARK

I should know better though. And sometimes I
interrupt people because I'm so keen to have my
say.
Silly because I hate it when people do it to me.

                    DAVE

At least you know you're doing it. And it could be
worse. You could do that really irritating thing
when you …

                    MARK

… Finish someone's sentence for them?

                    Dave

That's the one.

Manners matter

Listening to others properly is just plain good manners. Do manners have anything to do with being interesting? Of course they do.

All cultures have developed sets of manners and accepted rules of behaviour towards others. They are there to manage our everyday behaviour and to help us get the most out of our interactions and communications with the people around us.

Showing manners means respecting others. If we don't respect them, they won't respect us. Without respect we will not be interesting.

To be interesting we need to be able to communicate, interact and connect with people. If we are rude, arrogant, boorish and don't know how to behave, we are unlikely to communicate or connect.

In *The Advancement of Learning,* Francis Bacon (1561–1626), the English philosopher, statesman and author, defined manners like this:

> "The whole of decorum and elegance of manners seem to rest in weighing and maintaining with an even balance, the dignity betwixt ourselves and others."

If manners maketh man, then manners help maketh man interesting.

66 Leadership expert Major Chris Whipp told me of an experience he had when coaching a senior business figure on leadership skills. The guy was just not getting it so Chris stopped the session and pointed through the window to a woman – "tell me about that woman" said Chris. "What do you mean?" said the man. "Does she have children? What are their names? What car does she drive? Where does she go on holiday?" "I don't know" replied the man. "Why don't you know?" asked Chris. "Because I'm not interested" came the reply. "Then you'll always be a manager – you will never be a leader" said a very disappointed Chris. 99

- *Dave*

66 One of the most important attributes that leaders possess is about how they interact with those they lead. The dominant strength that leaders possess over managers is the ability to develop their team, to encourage them to realize their potential. By knowing their staff and understanding what it is that makes their team members tick – their strengths and weaknesses, their dreams and desires, their values and beliefs – a leader is able to have a positive influence. By recognizing that they are all individuals and giving them a united purpose, a leader creates an environment of development and success. How does a leader do this? Well, in very simple terms, by asking questions, talking to their staff and, perhaps more importantly, listening. The real reason people are interested in leaders is because leaders are interested in people. 99

- *Major Chris Whipp*

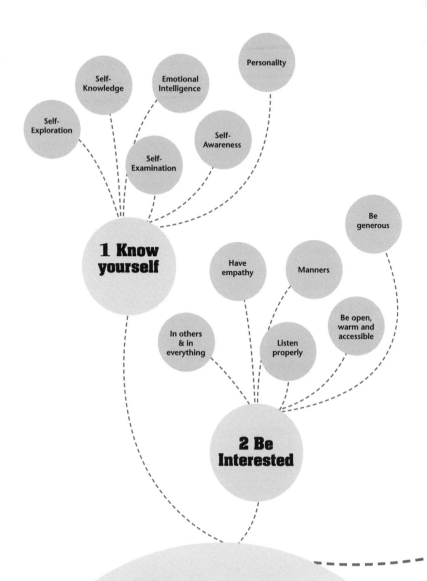

Self-Exploration

Self-Knowledge

Emotional Intelligence

Personality

Self-Examination

Self-Awareness

1 Know yourself

Have empathy

Manners

Be generous

In others & in everything

Listen properly

Be open, warm and accessible

2 Be Interested

How to be interesting

3 Be enquiring

A few questions before we move on

What, in many ways, is the most important character on a computer keyboard?

Here are a few clues. Is it a letter? No.

Is it a number? No.

Is it a punctuation mark? Yes. Any ideas?

Need any more clues? We've used it six times on this page already.

Yes, that's right it's … the question mark. The ?

Who? What? Where? When? Why and How? They would not be complete without it.

Why is the question mark so important?

Because we, as humans, have enquiring minds. We like to ask questions. Why? Because we are always in search of answers.

Why does the moon orbit the earth?

Why do some trees lose their leaves in autumn?

Why do we laugh and cry?

The more questions we ask, the more answers we will get. And the more answers we have, the more we know. And knowledge makes us interesting.

For the sake of being interesting, an obsolete word for the question mark is an eroteme.

"Creativity is a great motivator because it makes people interested in what they are doing. Creativity gives hope that there can be a worthwhile idea. Creativity gives the possibility of some sort of achievement to everyone. Creativity makes life more fun and more interesting."

Edward de Bono

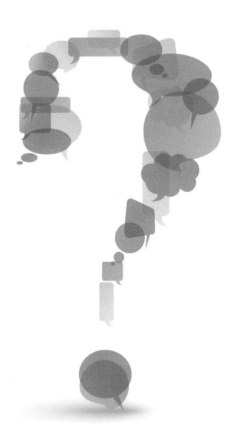

A creative mind is made of questions

Now here is a beautiful piece of insight into why questions and an enquiring mind are intrinsically linked to creativity.

Creativity is one of humanity's most potent powers that helps make us interesting.

It's from Dave Trott – advertising legend, creative director of countless great ad campaigns and author of *Creative Mischief* (a very interesting read, written by a very interesting man).

A creative mind is an enquiring mind

I recently went to a talk at The Science Museum.

Stephen Hawking, James Dyson, Robert Winston and Richard Dawkins.

Four people who range from merely brilliant to genius.

What I loved best was, as they talked, these brilliant men changed into little boys.

They were bubbling over with fun and playfulness and eagerness to ask questions about the world.

To discover everything they could about their environment.

Dying to share what they'd found out about how things work.

Full of questions and excitement.

Just the way a little child is knocked out just to be alive.

James Dyson talked about how Frank Whittle invented the jet engine before the Second World War.

And if the government had only listened we could have had jet planes fighting the Luftwaffe in The Battle of Britain.

Robert Winston talked about his medical hero.

Who, around 1780, had been able to remove a tumour twice the size of the man's head.

Without anaesthetic and without disfigurement.

Predating plastic surgery by nearly 200 years.

Richard Dawkins talked about the man who discovered natural selection at the same time as Darwin.

But humbly gave Darwin all the credit.

It was riveting to listen to these people because they loved what they did.

Dry, dull, academic subjects like science, chemistry and biology came alive.

And gradually it dawned on me what they all had in common.

They all had enquiring minds.

And I realized I was watching not only four very brilliant people.

But four creative people.

Because that's what makes people creative.

An enquiring mind.

As de Bono says: "There are many people calling themselves creative who are mere stylists."

And what separates the creative people from stylists is an enquiring mind.

Not just people who want to reshape or restyle an existing solution.

But people who say, "Why does it have to be that way?"

People who question the question.

People for whom the "?" at the end of a sentence is the most important part of the sentence.

I loved the energy, the buzz, the vitality, the aliveness.

The sense of discovery.

Not just rehashing what other people have done and trying to do it slightly better.

Questioning the very basis of what's being done.

Seeing it doesn't have to be done that way.

The thrill of upsetting accepted wisdom.

Discovering a new way.

A way no one else had found.

Or a way everyone else said wouldn't work.

That's true creativity.

And those four scientists/inventors/philosophers had it coming off them like sparks.

Asking what every creative person should always be asking.

"Why?"

Interesting people ask interesting questions

Part of the human condition is our curiosity. Who? What? When? Where? Why? How? Are the questions that spawn an infinite number of other questions when we add something to them. Thinking in this way adds interest to situations, conversations and people.

> "When you're curious, you find lots of interesting things to do."
>
> **Walt Disney**

Interesting people ask interesting questions. But what sort of questions are they? Interesting people ask questions of others and themselves. Interesting people ask questions and find answers.

Why not count how many questions you ask in a day? And before you do, have a guess at how many you'll ask. It'll be interesting to know how close you are.

Who? What? When? Where? Why? How?

Who?

Who am I? Who do I want to be? Who do people think I am? Who loves me? Who cares? Who finds me interesting? Who do I like? Who do I care about? Who do I fancy? Who do I find interesting?

What?

What do I think? What do I know? What matters to me? What is my opinion? What makes me sad? What makes me laugh? What makes me curious? What do I believe? What interests me?

When?

When do I think best? When have I felt great? When did I think of someone else? When was I unhappy? When did I last laugh? When did I last cry? When is the best time?

Where?

Where do I come from? Where do I belong? Where am I going? Where do I want to be? Where do I want to be in my career? Where are we in this relationship? Where to now?

Why?

Why do I think that? Why did I say that? Why did I behave in that way? Why do I feel like this? Why don't I do more? Why would I care? Why don't I take more interest? Why ... oh why ... oh why?

How?

How are you? How do I feel about that? How do you think it went? How do I look? How can I be more effective? How can I get their attention? How can I be more interesting?

This may look like a jumble of questions but they are all questions we have asked ourselves at some point in our lives. If we didn't constantly ask questions we would not be interesting people.

How to be interesting in job interviews

Interviews are all about questions. But you won't get anywhere if you just leave the interviewer to do all the questioning.

The whole interview process is about discovering who that person is and whether or not they are interesting. If two people interviewed have identical qualifications, the person deemed to be more interesting would always get the job.

The clever interviewee won't just answer the questions of the interviewer; they will take an interest themselves and ask questions of their own. If they don't it could send the negative message that they are not really that bothered about getting the job.

People are rarely given jobs purely based on the fact that they are capable of doing the work. We select people we like and liking people generally means that we find them interesting. The more interesting people are, the bigger the chance of their being employed.

Placing interesting people in interesting jobs

James Reed, Chairman of recruitment giant Reed, knows a thing or two about interesting people. James has built a business around placing interesting people in interesting jobs.

You might expect someone like James Reed to be rather gloomy about the current job situation in a double-dip recession, but he is adamant that in tough times people can be very resourceful, creative, innovative and interesting as a result of their circumstances.

He says that it is never easy to know what skills are going to be required from potential employees in five years' time, but he knows the kind of people that his organization would like to place in jobs. Those people have "curiosity, energy, vitality, integrity". So, determined to get this process right, Reed, together with Dr Paul Stoltz, created the 3G Mindset – a new assessment and validating guideline for interviewing. To James Reed the mindset is just as important as the skill set. He feels that it is important for people to be seen to be interesting when in the job market. Employers like to hire people who have enquiring minds that are able to look at business issues from different angles – or indeed employees that are entertaining and good to have around the office.

Reed is the kind of person who embraces change and is constantly on the lookout for new developments and new thinking – "if the bus is going somewhere interesting, I want to be on it" he said "my worry is that I might be walking home!"

A meeting of minds

Meetings can be fascinating pieces of human interaction. They can throw up all sorts of new and creative ideas. They can problem solve. They can re-direct focus. They can change the course of a business and bring it more success.

They can also have a negative effect. They might be point-scoring opportunities for rivals. There are often multiple agendas that vary from the official one. Sometimes there are people who simply do not wish to be there. There can be those who try to dominate. Others who withdraw and say nothing. They can be hijacked. They may be sabotaged.

Meetings can be an absolute minefield of confusion. They can also be pleasant and illuminating.

Not knowing what we might be walking into is often difficult. So how can we be interesting in meetings? It's a tough one. Probably the best thing we can do is be as well prepared as we possibly can and look upon the meeting as an opportunity to create a positive change.

If there is nothing positive to say, probably best say nothing. We don't have to talk for the sake of making our voice heard. Some people talk too much, which can have the effect of keeping others quiet who actually may have had something interesting to say.

Very often there are people in meetings who don't say anything, they sit and listen. Let's not be too quick to write them off as uninteresting or not being interested. They might be soaking up all the information to take away, digest and use in an interesting and productive way. Their interesting contribution to that meeting may well come later.

Isn't being interested in meetings about being open-minded, prepared, up-beat and focused?

That was my wife... our hamsters had babies!!

Givers are much more interesting than takers

Many people really dread networking events where they have to mingle with people they don't know and hopefully be engaging enough for people to be interested in them.

This is where knowing who we are and what our brand is becomes really important. This is also where our ability to listen to other peoples' stories matters. Interesting people recognize that such events are effectively trade-offs and the unwritten rule is that personal information is best shared as equally as possible.

How big can a network get? Is it possible to judge how interesting a person is by the extent of their personal network? Ever heard anyone say:

"She's really interesting – she knows everybody!"

Does "knowing everybody" make us interesting? It possibly shows that having an extensive personal network means a lot of people have taken an interest in someone. For that to be really true though, the network has to be continually working. There is little point in "knowing everybody" if we don't communicate with them.

Probably the most interesting and productive way of stimulating interest in ourselves is by increasing the network of other people. Being the glue that brings people together is a very clever way of remaining interesting to our personal network and keeps us at the front of people's minds.

Givers are much more interesting than takers. Working our network in this way can result in legions of contacts out there constantly referring to brand us and all we have done is help them get connected. How interesting is that!

> **"** Back in the bad old days of theatre when young actors had to get an Equity Card before they could work properly, I was lucky enough to be given mine for playing the back end of the cow in *Jack and the Beanstalk* at *The Theatre Royal Stratford East.* Meanwhile, up the road from our production, my friend Colin Wakefield was playing the back end of the cow in *Jack and the Beanstalk* at the *Palace Theatre in Watford.* The Stage *newspaper decided to publish an article entitled* A Tale of Two Jacks *comparing the two productions. In this article their cow was deemed to be more interesting than ours because it had four university degrees – on for each hoof! I tell you – it's pretty demeaning to be considered so uninteresting and come second in a two cow race!* **"**

- Dave

It's not a science. There is no secret formula.

It's good to be different

It's good to think differently about things sometimes. It's good to do things differently too. A different approach means a fresh new way of looking at things. It helps make us interesting.

Open your mind with maps

Mind mapping is a really smart way to plan out one's thinking on a subject or theme. The expression "mind map" was first made popular by British psychology author Tony Buzan.

It's a graphic plan using images and text that combines all the elements of the subject or theme into one diagram representing ideas, concepts, relationships, associations and flow. It typically starts with an oval, circle or other shape in the middle and the concept or thought to be explored is written inside the shape.

You will probably have noticed our mind map in creation throughout this book. We've been using it to assemble and order our thoughts. And to build up a picture of what it is to be interesting.

When creating a mind map we often find that adding one element to the map immediately gives us another thought, so that the mind map grows organically. Sometimes it's as if the mind map builds itself.

Mind mapping is more intuitive and less hierarchical than writing a list. And because it uses visual elements, like shapes, lines, symbols and scribbles, it can make it easier to get your head around a problem, as well as inspire more branches of ideas and thoughts.

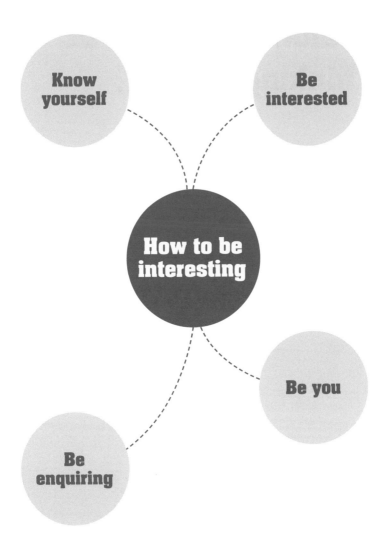

The next page has been left intentionally blank. Think of it as thinking space...

Have ideas

(Lots of them and share your ideas with others)

INT. STUDY.DAY

Dave and Mark at their desks.

> DAVE
>
> So the more people actually do, the more interesting
> ~~they are likely to be. And if we don't do much, just~~
> slob around all the time, people are less likely to
> ~~find us interesting? Is that what we're saying?~~

> MARK
>
> I think so yes. Funny you should mention that
> because I was chillaxing on the sofa last night,
> vegetating in front of the TV …

> DAVE
>
> Mark?! Did you just say "chillax"?

> MARK
>
> Yep.

> DAVE
>
> I cannot believe that you just said the word "chillax".
> ~~That's not a word that a grown man should use.~~

> MARK
> (smiling)
> ~~I know. I just wanted to see how you would react.~~
> I knew someone at university who liked to learn a
> ~~new word every day.~~

> DAVE
>
> Nerd?

> MARK
>
> ~~Not at all. Really interesting man. His favourite book~~
> was the dictionary. Guess what he used to say about it?

> DAVE
>
> What?

> MARK
>
> "As books go it's not much of a story but it
> ~~explains itself as it goes along."~~

Explo**Q**re
language.
L♥ve
words.

**Our use of language makes us interesting.
Experiment and play with it.**

> ❝ *Petra Ni is a former EU translator and multi-lingual project manager. She speaks Finnish, Swedish, Dutch, French and English. She thinks that learning other languages makes us interesting because it gives us a chance to see the world from another point of view.*
>
> *She told me that every language conveys a culture that is different to our own. So when we learn a new language, it helps us to not only understand other nationalities better but to also gain a more profound sense of our own culture.*
>
> *As Charlemagne put it around 800 AD "to have a second language is to have a second soul". That made me think of Nelson Mandela's view: that if you talk to a man in a language he understands, that goes to his head; if you talk to him in his language, that goes to his heart.* ❞
>
> *- Mark*

Learn a new word every day

It makes us interesting and it's quick and easy to do. To get you started, here are next week's new words. If some of them aren't new to you, you know where the dictionary is. If none of them are new to you, we're very impressed.

Kleptocracy - government by thieves

Grue - a shiver or shudder; a creeping of the flesh

Quercine - having the characteristics of or pertaining to oak.

Delenda - things to be deleted or destroyed

Gardyloo - old warning cry used in Edinburgh when throwing water or slops from a window.

Maunder - to move, talk or act aimlessly or incoherently

Mlit - fish sperm

Twit - a pregnant goldfish

This one is a popular urban myth – if you don't believe us, look it up on the web. Fish, as we all know, lay eggs so they can't become pregnant.

Being interested in other people means not only listening to what they say, but putting yourself in their shoes; this display of empathy not only shows that you're attentive but helps you to develop and broaden your emotional responses. It's hardly surprising that interesting people often read a lot of books – the experience of occupying a fictional world and seeing things from another perspective is one of the most creative things you can do with your time. It's also enormous fun.

The BBC in Britain conducted the Big Read survey of books  in 2003, the top 30 of which you'll see here. Yes, this list was compiled a while back now but is well worth exploring. Reading any of these books can help make us interesting. If you've read them all, we're jealous.

1. The Lord of the Rings, JRR Tolkien

2. Pride and Prejudice, Jane Austen

3. His Dark Materials, Philip Pullman

4. The Hitchhiker's Guide to the Galaxy, Douglas Adams

5. Harry Potter and the Goblet of Fire, JK Rowling

6. To Kill a Mockingbird, Harper Lee

7. Winnie the Pooh, AA Milne

8. Nineteen Eighty-Four, George Orwell

9. The Lion, the Witch and the Wardrobe, CS Lewis

10. Jane Eyre, Charlotte Brontë

11. Catch-22, Joseph Heller

12. Wuthering Heights, Emily Brontë

13. **Birdsong,** Sebastian Faulks

14. Rebecca, Daphne du Maurier

15. **The Catcher in the Rye,** JD Salinger

16. The Wind in the Willows, Kenneth Grahame

17. **Great Expectations,** Charles Dickens

18. Little Women, Louisa May Alcott

19. **Captain Corelli's Mandolin,** Louis de Bernieres

20. War and Peace, Leo Tolstoy

21. **Gone with the Wind,** Margaret Mitchell

22. Harry Potter and the Philosopher's Stone, JK Rowling

23. **Harry Potter and the Chamber of Secrets,** JK Rowling

24. Harry Potter and the Prisoner of Azkaban, JK Rowling

25. **The Hobbit,** JRR Tolkien

26. Tess of the D'Urbervilles, Thomas Hardy

27. **Middlemarch,** George Eliot

28. A Prayer for Owen Meany, John Irving

29. **The Grapes of Wrath,** John Steinbeck

30. Alice's Adventures in Wonderland, Lewis Carroll

Which of these would be your favourite five?

👓 *The votes could only be cast for novels, so the plays of Shakespeare were not included in the survey.*

Shared interests are common ground

Having common interests makes us interesting to others. That's why, in conversation, smart people quickly find a common interest to discuss. They make good opportunities for sharing information and enable us to find out more about each other and what else we have in common.

What makes TV chat shows interesting?

Television chat shows or talk shows are aired around the world.

The most popular shows generally feature interviews with celebrity guests. They usually talk about their work, their personal lives and the latest projects they are promoting.

Late night talk shows like *The Tonight Show* with Jay Leno and *Late Show with David Letterman* have been appearing on TV in the USA for years. The tried and tested formula of celebrity guest interviews, comedy sketches and audience participation is clearly a winner.

Viewers tune in to these shows time and time again because they find the guests interesting and want to find out more about them.

But they also watch the show because of the appeal of the host, who they're just as interested in. Indeed, often viewers are more interested in the host than the guest.

Great chat show hosts in Britain like Terry Wogan, Sir David Frost, Sir Michael Parkinson, Jonathan Ross and Graham Norton seem to have an effortless ease with their guests. They ask great questions and, more importantly, are superb listeners.

Graham Stuart is executive producer of *The Graham Norton Show* and co-founder of So Television, the company he set up with Graham Norton. He's a very interesting man. The show first screened on BBC 2 in 2007 and moved to BBC 1 in 2009. Series 12 started in 2012. Norton has interviewed a galaxy of famous names. His guest list over the years is a veritable A to Z of stars, from Tori Amos and Gillian Anderson to Robin Williams and Elijah Wood, from Cameron Diaz and Rod Stewart to Dame Judy Dench and Sir Patrick Stewart.

Here's what Graham Stuart says about Graham Norton and the show:

66 *I have to say that all of the guests we have on the show are extremely interesting in their own right. What makes them more interesting is Graham. His senses are razor sharp. His ability to listen and switch focus in order to generate an energy that carries guests and audience along is astonishing. No one is left out – audience or guests – Graham makes it an ensemble piece. Highly talented people like Graham have the ability to listen, absorb and respond rapidly.* 99

The intrigue of finding out about others

There's a much loved radio talk show which can give us some insight into how to be interesting. It's part radio programme, part national treasure.

Desert Island Discs was first broadcast on 29 January 1942 and has become one of the longest-running radio programmes in the world. It was devised by Roy Plomley, who originally presented the show, followed by Sir Michael Parkinson between 1985 and 1988, then Sue Lawley until 2006. It has been presented by Kirsty Young since 2006.

For anyone who has been living on a real desert island and doesn't know the programme, the format is brilliantly simple.

Every week a castaway guest chooses eight pieces of music, a book and a luxury item to take with them for their stay on a desert island.

The pieces of music are played while the guests discuss their reasons for their choices and what they mean in their lives.

So what is the universal appeal of the programme? The music is obviously an important part but so too is the fact that it features people we find interesting, sharing an aspect of their lives with the listener.

Desert Island Discs has endured for so long because it gives us a great opportunity to find out a little more about people we find interesting. And guests like to appear on it because, as we've said before, we all like talking about ourselves – it's the subject we know best.

By the time of the 70th anniversary of the programme, music by the Beatles had been chosen in 256 episodes.

What if you were on *Desert Island Discs*? What would your choice of music and luxury item be? Think carefully about this, particularly the luxury item. It can be pretty lonely on a desert island, so it had better be something interesting!

A random selection of guests with their choice of book and luxury item. We haven't the room to list their music choices. Why not find out for yourself?

Guest Arlene Phillips — Book Little Women by Louisa May Alcott — Luxury item Tweezers

Guest Paul Weller — Book One Hundred Years of Solitude by Gabriel Garcia Marquez — Luxury item Hot lemon flannels as provided in Chinese restaurants

Guest Felix Dennis — Book Absolute Beginners by Colin Macinnes — Luxury item A large pot of French Mustard

Guest Suggs — Book An Indian paper edition of Homer — Luxury item A settee to sit on

Guest Paul O'Grady — Book A concise book of Italian verbs — Luxury item A nucleus of bees

Guest J K Rowling — Book SAS Survival Guide — Luxury item Pen and unlimited paper

Guest Alison Steadman — Luxury item Skin So-Soft by Avon

Guest Boris Johnson — Book The Borrowers by Mary Norton — Luxury item Video camera and film

Guest Jane Horrocks — Book The Dictionary of National Biography

Guest Joanna Lumley — Book A huge atlas — Luxury item A very long stainless steel shaft to encourage pole-dancing mermaids

Guest Kelly Holmes — Book A set of encyclopaedias — Luxury item A large supply of chocolate

Book Jamie's Dinners: The Essential Family Cookbook by Jamie Oliver — Luxury item An endless supply of tissues

Guest Vivienne Westwood   Book A la Recherché du Temps Perdu by Marcel Proust   Luxury item Multi-lingual dictionary

Luxury item A pair of swimming goggles with prescription lenses

Guest Whoopee Goldberg   Book Letters to a Young Poet by Rainer Maria Rilke   Luxury item Wise potato chips

Guest Frank Warren   Book Treasure Island by Robert Louis Stephenson   Luxury item A set of different fragrances from the people she loves

Book The works of Rumi, Persian poet and philosopher   Luxury item A biography of Audrey Hepburn

Guest Darcey Bussell   Book A biography of Audrey Hepburn   Luxury item Merlot grapevine

Book A dictionary   Luxury item A karaoke machine   Luxury item An eyelash curler

Guest Chris Evans   Guest Brand

Guest Mary Portas

Guest Bob Geldof

Guest Brenda Blethyn

Book The Diary of Samuel Pepys   Luxury item Metropolitan museum in New York

Guest David Frost   Book The London A–Z   Luxury item Sunday newspapers   Luxury item A church organ

Book The History of the Decline and Fall of the Roman Empire by Edward Gibbon   Luxury item An anchored yacht

Guest George Clooney   Book War and Peace by Leo Tolstoy   Luxury item A cyanide pill

Guest Lyn Barber   Book The Complete F Scott Fitzgerald

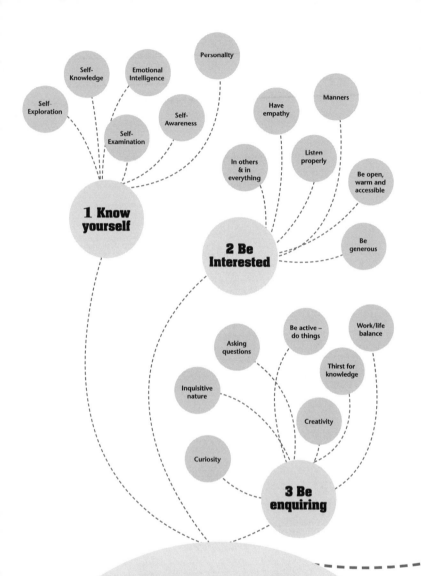

Self-Exploration

Self-Knowledge

Emotional Intelligence

Personality

Self-Examination

Self-Awareness

Have empathy

Manners

In others & in everything

Listen properly

Be open, warm and accessible

Be generous

1 Know yourself

2 Be Interested

Asking questions

Be active – do things

Work/life balance

Inquisitive nature

Thirst for knowledge

Curiosity

Creativity

3 Be enquiring

How to be interesting

4
BE YOU

THE INSTITUTE OF
CHARTERED LION TAMERS
ESTABLISHED BY ROYAL CHARTER IN 1880

The Vocational Guidance Counsellor sketch

Television's *Monty Python's Flying Circus* once ran a sketch called The Vocational Guidance Counsellor. It has been credited with giving accountancy a reputation for being dull and boring. Not a view we hold with, we might add.

A Mr Anchovy, played by Michael Palin, comes to see the Vocational Guidance Counsellor, played by John Cleese, about a possible change of career.

The Counsellor informs Anchovy that the results from the aptitude tests he took last week give a clear picture of the sort of person he is and that chartered accountancy is the ideal job for him.

Anchovy replies that he is a chartered accountant already and has been for the last twenty years. He explains that he wants a new job – something exciting.

"Chartered accountancy is exciting isn't it?" the Counsellor enquires.

Anchovy disagrees and tells him that it's dull, dull, dull.

The Counsellor explains that from Anchovy's report he can see he's an extremely dull person, which in chartered accountancy is not a disadvantage. In fact it's very beneficial.

Anchovy refuses to give up. He wants a new job. He wants to be a lion tamer.

The Counsellor gently cautions that a move from chartered accountancy to lion taming in one go might be rather drastic. He advises instead that perhaps Anchovy should work his way towards lion taming via banking.

You can catch this on YouTube or a DVD.

That's an interesting job

People often judge others by what they do for a living rather than who they are. It's an easy trap for us all to slip into.

Lion taming seems an interesting profession, so lion tamers must be interesting.

And accountancy seems a boring profession, so accountants must be boring. Not necessarily. In fact, not at all.

We both know many people in accountancy and finance who are far from boring. They are entertaining, knowledgeable individuals who are great company to be with and very interesting.

We don't actually know of any boring lion tamers; in fact we don't know any lion tamers at all. But we do know people with so-called "interesting jobs" that are not interesting as people in the slightest. I'm sure you do too.

We can all be interesting whatever the job and whether we work or not. People don't stop being interesting when they retire. One could suggest that with all the knowledge and wisdom they've acquired with age they are probably more interesting than they were when they were younger. A point we discuss elsewhere in the book.

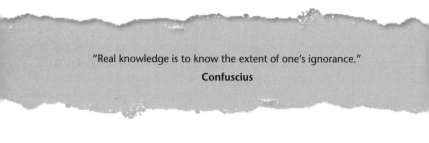

"Real knowledge is to know the extent of one's ignorance."
Confuscius

Be happy in yourself

What's your story?

The really great communicators recognize that every piece of communication is a story. We all have a personal story. Our story is who we were, who we are and who we might become. Stories are at the very heart of the human condition.

What sort of story are we? Adventure, thriller, love, tragedy, comedy, fairy tale, mystery – or a combination of the lot?

How do people tell their stories?

Interesting people tend not to force their stories upon us, they let us into their stories in episodic form. Charles Dickens did this brilliantly well with buyers of his periodical publications aching for the next installment. Getting to know someone can be a wonderful experience. Putting the pieces of the puzzle together as their story unfolds. It can be a pleasant surprise. It could be a shock. It will always be interesting.

> **❝** *One of my first TV jobs was playing Duncan the curate in EastEnders. A regular job and Albert Square became my home for a year or so. I enjoyed talking to everyone involved with the show: make-up, camera, writers, producers and extras. There was one particular extra, or should I say background artist, that I found especially interesting – her name was Maggie. Maggie took her job very seriously indeed. She had created a character with a complete family history. One day a new young director arrived to take charge of an episode. We were filming exteriors in the square and he needed some background activity for a particular shot. He called Maggie over – "what I want you to do, love, is to come into the back of this shot, walk up the steps of number 23 and ring the bell – okay?" "No." Replied Maggie. "What do you mean no?" Asked the rookie director. "We fell out with that lot years ago!" She said. Now, is it the interest or the Devil that is in the detail?* **❞**
>
> *- Dave*

Let's think about presentations for a moment

A presentation is all about the story and how well we tell it. When we heard the words "once upon a time" as children we knew that we were off on an adventure – we were interested. The problem with growing up is that we somehow feel that it is not cool to make business presentations stories.

"No. This is a serious presentation where I am presenting hard facts with home truths so you'd all better sit up and listen!"

Just making this up, but it sounds like the sort of thing that might have been said.

Maybe this is more familiar:

"I work in an analytical world – I don't have time to tell stories, I've just got to tell it as it is."

That wasn't made up.

Every piece of communication is a story of some sort or has a story behind it. Stories bring order to chaos. They put things in perspective. Stories have themes, moods and characters. Stories stir emotions. Stories make us think.

When creating a presentation it might be a good idea to decide what kind of story it is – for instance, in the world of finance at the moment there are probably a lot of horror stories around! Losing a client – keeping in touch – getting the client back is definitely a love story with a happy ending! There are many more familiar themes that can reach out to us in the form of a presentation. One thing is for sure – the message will be interesting and memorable.

Christopher Booker's *The Seven Basic Plots* gives us a really good heads up on what we can employ to make our stories hit the spot. Booker believes that there are seven basic plots:

1. Overcoming the Monster
2. The Quest
3. Voyage and Return
4. Tragedy
5. Comedy
6. Rebirth
7. Rags to Riches

Let's go back to horror stories in the financial world. There may be many finance directors and accountants out there who not only claim their material is dry and uninteresting but also that they have to deliver bad news and tough messages.

Here's a possible presentation scenario that the poor company accountant might have to deliver:

The figures do not make good reading. There has been no growth this year; in fact there has been a loss. There might be some light at the end of the tunnel and he has some ideas that could get things back on track.

Overcoming the Monster	He tells us of the do or die situation.
The Quest	It is certainly one of those.
Voyage and Return	There is a journey to be made and hopefully a return too.
Tragedy	No denying this is what the situation is.
Comedy	In a wry and ironic way you have to laugh or you would cry.
Rebirth	This is what is required.
Rags to Riches	That is what we are after.

See. This accountant is not as dull as he thought he was!

As any good actor will tell you, there's nothing more interesting than watching someone think

Am I interesting when I deliver my presentations?

Maybe we should ask ourselves if we look a little different compared to how we do usually and if that might signify the interest we have in what we are about to say. We are, after all, on show. Different clothes from those we might normally wear in our everyday business life or the clothes everyone has seen us wearing in the office all week might do the trick. Attention to how we look can signal that we believe what we have to say is important and interesting. It could also make us feel good about ourselves.

We are still children at heart and we never lose that interest in storytelling. Stories make business, social and domestic interaction interesting.

We have all asked ourselves if we come across as interesting when delivering presentations. Maybe the most assured way to be interesting is to know the story well and deliver it with the same degree of passion and enthusiasm with which we conceived and prepared it.

Isn't it about feelings? When we let people know how we feel about what we are saying, it is likely to gain their interest and possibly even change the way they feel about what is being said. If we make decisions about how we want people to feel at any given point during our presentation, we may well secure their interest. They might even carry those emotions out of the meeting room and pass the message on.

When we go to the theatre or the cinema or to listen to music or watch dance and movement, we are paying money in the expectation of having our emotions pulled in all sorts of directions. Perhaps we need to view our presentations in the same way. Feelings will influence opinion and decision.

Janet's talks on the subject of sex were legendary.

Perfect pitch

One of the best examples of how to be interesting in a presentation and how to make an interesting pitch is demonstrated in a superb scene from the award-winning TV series *Mad Men*.

Lead character, 60s ad agency man Don Draper, is pitching to Kodak to bag the campaign for their new slide machine that's being referred to as the wheel. He tells his story with words and pictures.

Draper makes the pitch personal to himself while showing slides of his estranged family – his wife and children.

Imagine the scene in the boardroom. The executives arrive and are seated. Draper stands up to present. The lights are dimmed. The Kodak slide machine starts. It shows a slide of Don Draper's family life.

Draper tells them that in Greek, "nostalgia" literally means "the pain from an old wound" and that it's a twinge in your heart far more powerful than memory alone.

While showing a series of slides of his family life in happier days, he explains that this new Kodak device isn't a spaceship but a time machine.

A time machine that goes backwards, forwards and takes us to a place where we ache to go again. "It's not called the Wheel" he says, "it's called a Carousel".

Draper ends the presentation by telling his audience that the carousel lets us travel the way a child travels. Around and around, and back home again ... to a place where we know we are loved. He shows his old wedding photograph.

This pitch is classic emotional investment and the very essence of great storytelling, which cannot fail to capture the interest of his potential client.

At the end of the pitch the looks on the faces of the guys from Kodak tell their own story. They are sold – the business is definitely won. Catch the scene on YouTube or invest in the box set. It's a classic.

COME ON, DON'T BE SHY

(But don't be a show-off either)

Being interesting is about being confident
but not over-confident.

Are interesting people confident, and are confident people interesting?

To be interesting it helps to be confident. Here's psychologist Michael Brooke's considered view on the link between how to be interesting and confidence.

Are we generally confident or is it something more specific to certain situations or skills? Where does confidence come from?

If we were to ask most people how important confidence is, especially in their work, they will usually rate this quality as pretty important. There aren't many situations where confidence is unhelpful. (Arrogance, on the other hand, is another matter!).

The world of professional sport is one area where confidence comes under close scrutiny. Narrow victories (where little separates performers physically) are often attributed to superior confidence in the victor. For this reason a ream of confidence research has been conducted in the sporting arena.

Asking people where confidence actually comes from elicits many different responses. Is it your parents, your coach, your manager, your environment, practice, encouragement, positive experiences?

The psychologist Professor Albert Bandura [1] is perhaps the most influential academic on this topic. He came up with the notion of self-efficacy (for self-efficacy, read confidence!).

Self-efficacy is about belief in one's ability to achieve a goal or task, i.e. to achieve a positive outcome. Bandura claimed there are four major sources of self-efficacy:

1. Past successes – Mastering a task strengthens our belief that we can do it, and we tend to be drawn to do things we are good at, and do them more! On the flip side, struggling or failure at a task or skill can lead to avoidance.

2. Modelling – Someone else performing well can add to our own belief we can do it too! An example: until Sir Roger Bannister completed the first four minute mile in 1954, it wasn't believed possible. Numerous people have since exceeded this time.

3. Persuasion (or feedback!) – Encouragement from others boosts confidence. Similarly, what we are saying to ourselves has an impact (our self-talk, the inner voice). Confident people tend to have a much more positive dialogue going on inside their heads. "I can do this, I've done this really well before."

4. Control over emotional/physical states – The brain and the body are linked; there's no getting away from it. Confident people tend to interpret physical stress/threat responses, such as increased heart rate and butterflies in the stomach, as positive signs of readiness to perform. Less confident folk (picture the over-nervous public speaker) might allow these physical symptoms to get the better of them. If you have ever forgotten your words when anxiously speaking in public, and then remembered them as soon as you've calmed down, you'll know what this feels like and will probably agree this is not a confidence-boosting experience.

More recently, researchers within high performance sport, e.g. Bull et al [2], have become interested not simply in having confidence, but in having stronger, more robust confidence. By this they mean a level of confidence that is not easily knocked by a setback.

The route to robust confidence is understanding where confidence comes from in the first place, and working constantly and deliberately to strengthen the four sources.

So, if confidence increases "interestingness", we might want to increase our confidence. According to what we've been discussing, the solution is to spend time building up the four sources of confidence. Looking at each, we could start with a few simple steps using the four sources of self-efficacy:

(Source 1) Remind ourselves of what we've achieved, regularly.

(Source 2) Model ourselves on those we admire – what are they doing well that we can emulate?

(Source 3) Get into the habit of seeking feedback from others – if it's positive, bank it. If it's negative, act on it to get better. (The more specific the feedback, the better.) Also, speak to ourselves! Is our inner voice a helpful, friendly coach, or a negative, nit-picking critic? Somewhere in the middle of these two is the aim.

(Source 4) Practise some of the numerous techniques available that can help us gain more control over our physical state at those moments when we know our nerves can get the better of us.

(1) Bandura, A. (1977). Self-efficacy: Toward a unifying theory of behavioural change. Psychological Review, 84: 191–215.

(2) Stephen J. Bull, Christopher J. Shambrook, Wil James and Jocelyne E. Brooks (2005). Journal of Applied Sport Psychology, 17: 209–227

Be yourself

You're the only person who can play that role.

Is that really me?

We will only secure genuine and sustained interest in ourselves if we are true to ourselves. Nobody likes a phoney. There really is no point trying to emulate someone we admire if we clearly do not have that person's attributes. "I am what I am. I am my own special creation" says the song.

The bottom line is – if we want to share ourselves with other people, it helps to know who we are.

Do I care?

Anyone who says, "I don't care what people think of me" is probably either a fool or a liar or possibly both. We should care. We should care very much. The trouble with not caring is that it will be perceived as a brand and that will be a brand that people will not wish to buy or associate with.

What's my brand?

Jeff Bezos, the founder of Amazon, said "Your brand is what people say about you when you are not in the room".

Our brand is how we are perceived and how we want to be perceived. If we do not create our brand someone else could do it for us. It might not be the one that we want.

BRANDS AND MAVERICKS

The word "brand" comes from brandr, the Old Norse word for "to burn."

It relates to companies burning their mark (or brand) onto their products.

But cattle were branded long before producers started branding their products. We all know the expression "a maverick" for someone who is fiercely independent or who likes to go their own way and not follow the crowd. Well, the term "maverick" originally referred to an unbranded calf.

Samuel Maverick was a Texas lawyer, politician and land baron in the 1800s. While other landowners branded their cattle, he decided not to.

This meant that any unbranded cattle a rancher found became known as mavericks. Some say he didn't brand his cattle because he thought it cruel; others say it was because he didn't care about ranching. Another theory for him not branding his cattle is that he could then claim any unbranded cattle as his own.

There's one little twist in this "interesting" diversion.

His grandson, US Congressman Maury Maverick, is credited as being the person who first coined the word "gobbledygook" to describe jargon or painfully convoluted language. Maury used the word when he was chairman of the US Congress Smaller War Plans Committee to criticize the obscure language used by other members of the committee.

What's your brand? Do you have one?

Launched in 2010, The Groucho Club Maverick Award is described as "the antidote to other awards". It recognizes those who have broken the mould in their field and made a significant contribution to culture and the arts in the previous 12 months. Danny Boyle, Nick Davies and Nell Gifford are past winners.

"Your most valuable asset is your brand …

… but it must have substance."

Wise words from Rita Clifton – an interesting person with an interesting background in an interesting industry.

Rita was London Chief Executive and then Chairman at Interbrand, the world's leading brand consultancy, from 1997 to 2012. Before that she was Vice Chairman and Strategic Director at Saatchi & Saatchi. She now has a portfolio of chairing and non-executive directorships, including Bupa, Nationwide, Dixons retail plc and Populus. Pro bono roles include the boards of WWF, the Henley Festival and chair of the leading environmental volunteering organization, The Conservation Volunteers. All-in-all, the ideal person to chat to about making personal brands interesting.

In Rita's opinion it is what is behind the façade that is important. She believes that it is all about who we are beneath the look. What we feel, how we think, what we believe, what our values are, what we feel strongly about.

We have to live our brand – it cannot be something we just put on when we think we need to. It is very much part of our DNA. It would be no good for a company to give off an image of being a bright open, exciting, breath of fresh air kind of outfit if its HQ was a series of dark, dingy, windowless rooms with closed doors off a gloomy corridor.

"The happiest people in this world are those who have the most interesting thoughts."
William Lyon Phelps

Who's that in the mirror?

The first step to discovering or creating our personal brand and generating the kind of interest we would like people to have in us is to take a good, hard look at ourselves.

Where do you come from?

What is your background?

What do you feel strongly about?

What do you wear?

What do you like to read?

What do you like to watch on TV?

What types of food do you enjoy eating?

What are your hobbies?

Etc. etc.

The list of questions we could ask ourselves is huge, but we should ask anyway.

When we have answers for all of these questions we should address those answers with whys.

What image am I portraying?

Our image is part of our brand. In fact our image is a key component of our brand. To be interesting in a way that others will wish to connect with us, a close inspection of the image we portray is necessary. Our image is physical, vocal and emotional. It is the very core of our brand.

How do I look?

The first point of interest is not necessarily how tall, short, wide, narrow or physically attractive we are but the signals our physicality sends out.

Apparently, posture and gesture account for around 50% of the messages we communicate. The old saying of not getting a second chance at a first impression is so true.

Long before anyone has made eye contact with us or hears the sound of our voice, they make a judgement on what they see – often subconsciously. Aloof and arrogant posturing is a turn off and will push people away. People do not gravitate with interest to cocky swaggerers who look down their nose.

By the same token, a timid, apologetic physicality will close us off and discourage interest. If we want people to be interested in us before they know very much about us, we need to send out the right physical signals.

An open and neutral posture makes us appear confident and accessible and allows people to approach us. This is the framework of our physical brand. Once that is established the flourishes of style and colour can be added to complete the physical statement.

Another of Oscar Wilde's great quotes was:

> "It is only shallow people who do not judge by appearances."

"Tonight folks I'll be playing both Randall and Hopkirk."

As a TV presenter and interviewer, Trish Lynch interviews hundreds of people every year. She notes that although it is her job to ensure the interviewee comes across as interesting by asking the right questions, if there is an energy or spark there to begin with, the questions become almost immaterial:

❝ *By an energy/spark I mean a sparkle in the eyes, a curiosity that shines through, a mischievous look that lets you know it's all going on in there. Eye contact is vital and there's not many people can maintain eye contact when put in an uncomfortable interview situation. Frequently, your knees are touching and your faces are a matter of inches away from each other for the camera angle. Keeping the contact going without staring is tricky and a skill we can all learn.*

In Ireland we frequently describe someone as having "smiling eyes". It doesn't always reach the mouth but that's the best kind of smile, as it can't be faked. It's infectious as it allows the other person to believe you find them interesting. Hey, we all love a bit of flattery, and thinking you are bowling the other person over with your charm, wit and personality can only be a good thing. Win–win.

Can you learn to be interesting? Absolutely, you just need to find out where to start and practise on everyone you meet.

Older people appear to have cornered the market on being stimulating company, in my opinion. That's not a coincidence either. They have had the time to try out different methods of getting what they want and hone it over time. Those that are born with the charisma gene are the lucky ones; life will most certainly be kind to them. Everyone else has to work at it, plain and simple, no short cuts.

To me, Being Interesting is a complex recipe of ingredients, that certain something that we just can't put our finger on. Start with smiling eyes, add in lots of questions for the other person (they will love it) and get a life. Simple! **❞**

"But darling, you couldn't be more interesting if you tried."

Smile and the world smiles with you

If someone smiles at us when we are walking down the street we tend to smile right back at them. We can't help it. Corny, but true.

A smile usually signifies interest – it connects us with the person who smiles back at us. It puts us in their mind. It may even make us wonder exactly why that person smiled at us.

Different kinds of smiles will send out different messages and feelings. The cheeky grin. The wry smile. The beam. The smug smirk. The coy smile. The flirty smile. The ironic smile. The resigned smile. The knowing grin.

The most famous smile, and some would say the most interesting smile, has to be on the face of the Mona Lisa – the enigmatic Giaconda smile. A smile that has inspired and intrigued. Writers, artists and poets the world over have been moved by Leonardo da Vinci's masterpiece.

Look at the painting. She's smiling at you. Why? What is she thinking? Why is she so interesting?

And keep laughing too

Humour is a very subjective thing – just like interesting is different things to different people, humour is the same. Slapstick, satire, observational, pantomime, silent, crude and black are all types of humour that have us rolling in the aisles. Humour must be one of the most interesting things to mankind.

And there are the other drug takers. The comics themselves! Junkies – every last one of 'em! Laughter, give me more of that laughter – I can't get enough of it! When comedians are able to extract laughter from their audience there is a feeling of worth, value, appreciation – interest. It's a different kind of drug but nonetheless potent.

Are comedians interesting because they make us laugh? Are they interesting because they want to make us laugh? Why do they do it? What's in it for them – besides the drug and money? As if that isn't enough … Is there a deeper reason?

Humour clearly plays a major part in our wellbeing. We are told that laughter provides a great health boost. It makes us feel good – gives us a high. We're all interested in feeling good. So, ipso facto, people who make us laugh must be of interest to us.

"To be compassionate one must have a sense of humour and be able to laugh at one's self."

- Lord Digby Jones, business leader and politician

Humour where you least expect it

We were in the Falklands in a combat situation supporting the Ghurkhas. It was freezing cold, wet, windy and dark. We had a navigational malfunction, which took us south of the lake instead of north, which led us into the middle of a minefield incurring serious casualties. We were being shelled but had to remain still for the next six hours while the Engineers cleared a path for us. It was a horrendous situation. Our radios were down and when the time came to move out, commands had to be passed verbally from Marine to Marine like Chinese whispers. "We're moving out" I said. This was then passed down the line. Suddenly I had an idea that would give extra safety to my men as they made their way out of the minefield ... "Place your feet in the footprints of the man in front of you." After about 10 seconds to my surprise my walkie crackled into life – it was Clark, my Corporal – "what kind of f.....g command is that? Have you seen the size of the bloke in front of me!!"

- Major General Andy Salmon CMG OBE, former Commandant General Royal Marines and General in NATO

How do I sound?

Does the sound we produce have a bearing on making what we say interesting? Apparently so.

Vocal production accounts for around 40% of the messages we communicate. As Peter Sellers said when mimicking Michael Caine's very distinctive voice on the *Parkinson Show* in the 70s, "Not many people know that!"

This is what actor and vocal coach Tessa Wood has to say about being vocally interesting.

Before looking at what makes a voice "interesting" it's important to recognize that there is a high degree of subjectivity in this area. All over the world people are forming relationships, falling in love and working with people possessing a vast range of voices, accents and levels of articulacy. The voice that to one will cause butterflies and breathlessness, to another will induce switch-off and sleep.

So what is an interesting voice, and how does it differ from a voice that is merely beautiful?

Quite simply, a voice that is "beautiful" can all too often be empty. People tend to like the sound it makes, but they don't actually connect to the content. In short – the balance is wrong. It's a bit like tuning a hi-fi or radio to be all bass instead of a balance. It makes an interesting sound, but it's almost impossible to absorb the whole message. So a voice can be beautiful but uninteresting. We need to hear the message.

I would argue that the interesting voice is one that has something interesting to say as a starting point. But of course, that isn't enough on its own. We have all sat through lessons, lectures and speeches that, whilst having an interesting core message, are communicated in a dull, sleep-

inducing way because of the speaker's voice. So an interesting voice needs to be a balance between sound and content.

If we take "something interesting to say" as our starting point, what other elements go towards making a voice sound interesting?

It's a bit like baking a cake; it's all about balance and getting a good mix of all the ingredients. By using a variety of pitch, tone, pace and volume we can add colour and texture to the sound we make.

It is a fact that virtually everyone is born with a good voice that has range, passion and projection. It is only as we go through life that we tend to move away from those things and constrain our natural sound.

It's also important to remember that our voice is the most outward manifestation of our innermost thoughts and feelings. It's a vehicle that allows those thoughts and feelings inside to travel out and be shared with others. Finding the voice that does that in the most positive, individual and compelling way cannot be anything other than interesting.

"And now for some sleight of hand..."

How do I feel?

This is where things get really interesting. We may not remember all of the words that are said to us but we never forget the way we have been made to feel. Feelings are what it is all about! When our curiosity has been roused, our brain begins the process of telling us how we feel. Many decisions are made after considering hard facts, but a great many more are made based on instinct and the emotions we are experiencing. We have often said and heard people say things like:

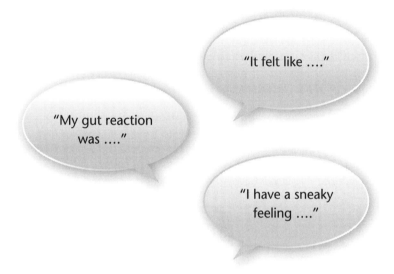

"It felt like ...."

"My gut reaction was ...."

"I have a sneaky feeling ...."

If we become interested in someone it may well be because they have something interesting to say and they might be saying it with a voice which pleases us – but there you are – we said it – pleases us. What kicks in to sustain our interest are our feelings. Most of this is subconscious but it's worth stepping back sometimes and analyzing exactly how we feel and why.

When babies develop and small children communicate, their entire response to any external stimulus is based on how they feel. They have the capacity to be curious, of course, but it is governed by emotion. If one baby cries in a room full of other babies, the rest will invariably join in. This is because they are empathizing – they are communicating the support they feel – they might not know it at the time but what other reason could there be? This behaviour carries on for some time even into adulthood. Some more familiar phrases:

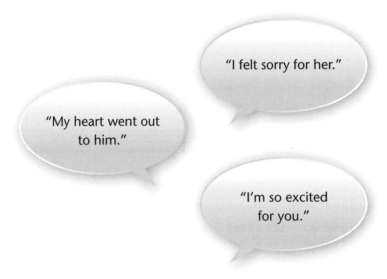

"I felt sorry for her."

"My heart went out to him."

"I'm so excited for you."

We would not say any of the above if we were not interested. Even negative feelings can be an extension of interest. Do we have to like someone to be interested in them? Probably not. It is very easy to be interested in some people that have committed horrendous atrocities without liking them. We are, however, likely to take a more sustained interest in people we like than those we don't.

So, the way we feel must play a big part in the interest we take and the interest we create.

Is your glass half full or half empty?

Are optimists more interesting than pessimists?

Are you a glass half full or glass half empty kind of person? If you are the former, a natural optimist, then it's highly likely that you'll be more interesting to others than if you are a pessimist.

Why? Well research seems to indicate that optimists tend to outperform pessimists in a myriad of ways. Optimists are more likely to try new things, be adventurous and welcome change.

This means that they build up more life experiences, which they can then go on to share with others.

Be an optimist – it will make you a more interesting person. That's not to say that there will not be occasions when it's sensible to be pessimistic.

Let's say you're on holiday on a beach. A lifeguard puts up a sign warning that it is "dangerous to swim today because of strong undercurrents". To think "it will be fine, I'll go for a swim anyway" is clearly optimism to the point of stupidity.

Far better to take a pessimist's view and decide not to swim (it is not worth the risk) but then be optimistic about circumstances changing for the better tomorrow and having a swim then.

But pessimists can have a tendency to drag us down and optimists are usually more fun to be with. We tend to spend more time with people who make us feel good.

An eternal optimist

❝ *An especially interesting person in my life was my grandfather on my mother's side of the family. Arthur Morgan was a supreme optimist. As far as Arthur was concerned there was always a silver lining to every dark cloud – literally! When my brother and I were young boys on holiday in Cornwall with parents and grandparents, the weather was often awful. Two boys with buckets and spades at the ready to take on a sunny day at the beach frequently opened the door to thunder and lightning and stair rods of rain. This, according to Arthur, was merely a bit of 'sea fret' that would dry up in no time at all. The next day would see an impenetrable blanket of fog masking any glimpse of daylight. Just a bit of 'heat haze', Arthur told us boys, that would disappear before we could say ice cream. Arthur gave us a lot of his time, and he put a fair amount of that time into making kites for us, which we ended up calling ground kites because we could never get them airborne. Ah … but one day, he told us, we would.* ❞

- Dave

Live
in the now

It's where all our opportunities and possibilities start.

There are many people who live in the past. There are also those who live in the future. Past and future will, of course, make up our story eventually, but being focused on the "now" is essential.

Sometimes it is a really good thing to focus totally on the "now" – experiencing to the full everything that is happening around us; appreciating, enjoying and being curious about things we might normally let pass over us. The detail. The colours, the shapes, the sounds, the smells, the energy, the life!

When we live in the "now" we live in interesting times. We are present, vital and engaged. We are interesting.

Watching good theatre or film is very much a "now" experience because the action is of the moment and it maintains our apprehension of what might happen next. We can, of course, be touched and moved by something that has happened in the past but it will never have the same impact as the "now"!

 Films give us stories to pass on to others. They can be a great topic for conversation, and can be enjoyed as art, as a way to relax, as a way to give your senses a thrill, or as a mystery to be solved.

Every ten years the American Film Institute takes a poll of the US film industry on the best films. Here's the top 50 from the last poll carried out in 2007.

1. Citizen Kane (1941)
2. The Godfather (1972)
3. Casablanca (1942)
4. Raging Bull (1980)
5. Singin' in the Rain (1952)
6. Gone with the Wind (1939)
7. Lawrence of Arabia (1962)
8. Schindler's List (1993)
9. Vertigo (1958)
10. The Wizard of Oz (1939)
11. City Lights (1931)
12. The Searchers (1956)
13. Star Wars (1977)
14. Psycho (1960)
15. 2001: A Space Odyssey (1968)
16. Sunset Boulevard (1950)
17. The Graduate (1967)
18. The General (1927)
19. On the Waterfront (1954)
20. It's a Wonderful Life (1946)
21. Chinatown (1974)
22. Some Like It Hot (1959)
23. The Grapes of Wrath (1940)
24. E.T. – The Extra-Terrestrial (1982)
25. To Kill a Mockingbird (1962)
26. Mr. Smith Goes to Washington (1939)
27. High Noon (1952)
28. All About Eve (1950)
29. Double Indemnity (1944)
30. Apocalypse Now (1979)
31. The Maltese Falcon (1941)
32. The Godfather, Part II (1974)
33. One Flew Over the Cuckoo's Nest (1975)
34. Snow White and the Seven Dwarfs (1937)
35. Annie Hall (1977)
36. The Bridge on the River Kwai (1957)
37. The Best Years of Our Lives (1946)
38. The Treasure of the Sierra Madre (1948)

39. Dr. Strangelove (1964)
40. The Sound of Music (1965)
41. King Kong (1933)
42. Bonnie and Clyde (1967)
43. Midnight Cowboy (1969)
44. The Philadelphia Story (1940)
45. Shane (1953)
46. It Happened One Night (1934)
47. A Streetcar Named Desire (1951)
48. Rear Window (1954)
49. Intolerance (1916)
50. Lord of the Rings: The Fellowship of the Ring (2001)

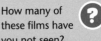 How many of these films have you not seen?

And just to throw them out there – some of our own top British films:

1. Don't Look Now (1973)
2. The Third Man (1949)
3. A Clockwork Orange (1971)
4. Get Carter (1971)
5. Whistle Down The Wind (1961)
6. Zulu (1964)
7. Chariots of Fire (1981)
8. The Long Good Friday (1980)
9. Four Weddings and a Funeral (1994)
10. Quadrophenia (1979)
11. Withnail & I (1987)
12. Gandhi (1982)
13. Kes (1969)
14. Billy Liar (1963)
15. The Go-Between (1970)
16. Nuts in May (1953)
17. Dead of Night (1945)
18. Local Hero (1983)
19. Saturday Night and Sunday Morning (1960)
20. The Ladykillers (1955)

How many of these have you seen? Were there any of them you really liked, or didn't like? If so, what made them interesting (or boring!)?

Try
new things

Albert Einstein, clearly a very interesting person, once said that "The person who never made a mistake, never tried anything new".

He also once said "E= mc^2", but neither of us ever really understood that to be honest. We've both tried numerous times, believe us, to get our heads around the energy, mass and the c-one (whatever that is?) equation. We are still none the wiser.

Change?

As François de la Rochfoucauld wrote in the 17th century "The only thing constant in life is change". And "Nothing endures but change" is credited to the Greek philosopher Heraclitus some 500 years before Christ. So no change there then.

Change is good. Change is interesting. Change happens.

From every piece of personal interaction change must happen. Change in circumstance. Change in feeling. Personal change. So do interesting people embrace change? Do boring people fear change?

Here's director, educationalist and communications coach Jim Dunk on how to be interesting and change:

To look at how to be interesting we must look at "change". It is my contention that all communication is entered into in order to bring about a change in the status quo. This does not need to be a large or momentous change, but all participants should emerge from a communication feeling that something has changed.

So, how do people interest me when I meet them as a coach? There are a number of early triggers. Do they really want to be there? Are they just obeying a directive from a manager, or do they have a genuine desire to find out something about themselves and achieve a "change" in their thinking or behaviour?

Coaching is more likely to be successful when the individual has a genuine desire to understand themselves and the ability to be truly self-critical in as honest a way as possible.

One of the most telling exercises is the consideration of the importance of Story as a means of communication. When people are asked to recall a favourite story from childhood and words like "surprise", "suspense", "variety", "humour", "scary", "creepy" are used, I know that the understanding of the power of storytelling is embedded and that the act of remembering is taking that person straight back to the childhood feeling and experience. Anyone who can become the child again through recalling how stories excited and changed them can begin to assemble the toolkit for changing the feelings of others.

When a group of people leaves a presentation or a meeting, the best "reading" of what has happened can be made by asking how they feel after the event. Again, one is looking for certain sorts of words: "inspired", "challenged", "empowered", "excited", "raring to go" and so on. This is the level of connection that is needed from successful communicators. Remember how memorable Barak Obama's assertion that "We can do it" was. There may be a lot of logistics and thinking to follow, but first one has to generate "the right feeling". Just like good storytelling.

People who aim for producing strong and positive feelings in their audiences will get a big return on their human investment. The need to capitalize on those feelings with good planning and action is obvious, but to try to change things without those feelings being engendered is a much harder task.

The "interesting" person is open to collaborative ways of working together and sharing any failures or successes. They are open, relaxed, confident, approachable and comfortable with themselves.

I am immediately "interested" by those people who arrive with a genuine desire to discover things about themselves, not only in Work, but also Family and the Life–Work Balance, and to find those areas that they wish to change. Through the changes they can make they will become better communicators and more productive, more effective, more interesting people.

66 Many years ago when I was working as a trainee manager in one of Nottingham's lace market factories, I had a wake-up call that changed my life. Every two or three weeks, Tony, the company rep, would show his face and drop off his orders. Tony was a typical "ladies man" of the time – moustache, curly perm, sovereign rings, sheepskin coat and absolutely reeking of Brut. I liked Tony and he seemed to take a shine to me and would often take me out for a lunchtime beer and a snack. I was young and pretty aimless at the time and he took an interest in me. "What do you do Dave?" He said on one of our Pie and Pint outings. "What do you mean?" said I. "What do you do when you're not at work?" "Not much – go to the pub with my friends sometimes." He looked at me and shook his head. "What are you doing with your life, lad? You can't just sit on your backside and wait for things to happen to you – you've got to go out there and make them happen!" That was probably the best kick up the bum I have ever had. Interesting people, like Tony, make things happen. 99

- Dave

More interesting with age

If knowledge and wisdom are linked to being interesting then, as we get older, we become more interesting, right? That should be the case. But it's often not seen that way.

Many years ago the Beatles wrote a song called "When I'm Sixty Four" – a song about being old. Ironically, being 64 in today's world isn't really thought of as being particularly old and the remaining Beatles are, in fact, now older than the subject of the song. The lyrics of the song throw up an interesting question:

> "Will you still need me? – will you still feed me?
> - when I'm sixty four?"

Will you still be interested in me? Is that what is being said?

We spoke to Dr Victoria Hill, a Consultant Clinical Psychologist who is a specialist in working with older people. Dr Hill had some interesting things to say about the older generation and how younger people might perceive them.

In her personal and her professional life Victoria says that she finds older people very interesting for a number of reasons. She feels interested in the fact that they grew up in quite a different world with different values and have seen so many changes and developments.

There is always a story, a past that might often be forgotten about rather than learnt from. She finds that they are generally more interested in others than perhaps younger generations are, which tends to manifest in a polite and enquiring type of behaviour and skills in good manners.

Are older people more interested in others and what is happening around them than younger generations?

Maybe – maybe not. Dr Hill does have one significant worry when it comes to the age gap, which takes us back to the lyrics of the song above. Do we care enough? In her work with older people in care homes she feels that old people are sometimes looked upon as a "walking diagnosis" and can be viewed as "a problem rather than a person". She thinks that not enough time is spent really getting to know who the person is.

Victoria also believes that when genuine interest is shown, a more pleasant atmosphere pervades and a win–win situation occurs for both carer and client. Her constant concern is that:

"Older people are often seen as a body rather than a somebody."

She is convinced that there is much to learn from older people and that perhaps their experience, their wisdom and their council is not sought enough from the generations below them. She says: "history teaches lessons – it's crazy not to consult the specialists!"

Age is just a number

This way
please

The fascination of leaders

❝ If people weren't interested in leaders, no one would ever follow them. Here's Major Chris Whipp on what makes leaders interesting:

Heads of State, military leaders, business leaders and captains of sports teams alike draw our attention. But leadership is a lot wider reaching than some might imagine; every parent, uncle and aunt is a leader.

Leadership is not about one's position in life, it is about how one acts in that given position. Leaders do so much more than just tell people what to do, and they are also more than just managers. They create a common goal, a journey, and they ensure their people are equipped for their specific role.

Leaders have a cause that they truly believe in. They have delved deep into their own self and discovered what is really important to them, what makes them tick. With this discovery they have made the very deliberate decision to commit. Passion is infectious; when we listen to someone speak on a subject that they are passionate about, it is engaging. We don't have to believe whatever it is they believe in, it is sufficient to believe that they believe it, which gets us interested in hearing their point of view. ❞

Leaders have a cause that they truly believe in. They have delved deep into their own self and discovered what is really important to them, what makes them tick. With this discovery they have made the very deliberate decision to commit.

Passion is infectious. When we listen to someone speak on a subject that they are passionate about, it is engaging. We don't have to believe whatever it is they believe in, it is sufficient to believe that they believe it, which gets us interested in hearing their point of view.

INT. SOUTHBANK CENTRE MEMBERS BAR.DAY

Dave and Mark look out of the window at the River Thames below. The sky is grey - the river a rich brown.

                          DAVE
    Shouldn't we talk a bit about connecting
    personally with people and leadership?

                          MARK
    You want to tell your Bill Clinton story again
    don't you?

> ❝ *I got a phone call one morning from a client at AOL. They were sponsoring an event at the O2 Arena at which Bill Clinton was speaking. I have always been a fan of Clinton as a speaker and communicator and these guys knew that.*
>
> *We were also writing a book called* The Clinton Factor *at the time and they knew that too. "Dave you've got to get yourself down to Greenwich, we've got a spare VIP ticket for the Clinton event!"*
>
> *I didn't need asking twice! Bill spoke with the same charismatic skill as he always did and we all hung on his every word. He had presence and knew how to make a great entrance. And although he was clearly a figure of leadership, he seemed able to connect with the audience on a personal level.*
>
> *After his keynote speech he fielded a few questions from the audience and then headed to the VIP enclosure for photos and chats.*
>
> *When he entered the room there was much excitement. He did what he was engaged to do and had his picture taken with each of us in turn and exchanged a few words in the process. I told him about the book and he kindly expressed his interest. That made me feel great.*
>
> *My overriding memory of that day is a strange one. There was an atmosphere that I have never felt before. It was as if all the men in the room wanted to be him, and all the women wanted to be with him.* ❞
>
> - *Dave*

Making business interesting – bringing richness from the outside

There is a school of thought that says that if we are first in to work and last to leave, work at the weekend, fill every waking hour with work, and demonstrate how busy we are, we will be productive, respected, appreciated, admired, even interesting. What is actually happening is that we are not enjoying and learning from everything else that is happening around us. Business is interesting, but it is probably more interesting when our experience of a broader existence brings richness from outside. To be interesting in business it helps to indulge in the "three Rs" – Rest, Recreation, Revitalization.

Speaking with one of the UK's leading business figures and an elected Lord was an interesting experience. As far as the three Rs go, Lord Digby Jones's wife, Pat, was happy to say that the man "… is a good relaxer and chills well!"

Digby himself said that their home in Warwickshire is the ideal place to catch up with family and entertain friends – but they do have to be interesting.

The divisional percentage of working life for Lord Jones is also interesting – 60% is taken up with paid business activity; 25% occupied by speaking engagements with businesses and educational establishments, interviews with the media and sessions in the House of Lords; 15% of his time is given to charitable organizations.

Digby is definitely of the school that great achievements aren't everything and that there are many people who have done a lot of brave, clever and creative things but are arrogant and pompous with it, and that is when the interest ends. He says the kind of people that interest him are provocative, humorous, caring and also interested. He believes that everyone has a story to tell and he is always eager to hear it. When invited to attend business functions or charity dinners he always asks the organizers to put him next to someone he doesn't know in order that he might be treated to a new story.

Having a strong point of view is also important to Digby – he told us that: "Men have walked up beaches and died so that we can publicly disagree."

He doesn't mind people disagreeing with his views provided that they are frank but not rude. In fact he welcomes healthy debate, of which he finds plenty in the House of Lords. Lord Jones has an interesting view on the members of both houses. He is of the mind that the members of the Lords are probably more interesting than those of the Commons because, "they tend to know what they are talking about!"

Very often successful business figures can be thought of as ruthless, unfeeling individuals who don't care who they step on to get to the top. It would be wrong to think of Lord Jones in this way, particularly in view of his belief in "socially inclusive wealth creation". It's an interesting look at the relationship that he feels business should have with the society it inhabits and the care that society deserves: "If people say they can't, it is incumbent on business to reach out, down, round and under to take people to a place where they can."

The Captains of Industry with a spring in their step and a smile on their face will undoubtedly draw interest. He or she can then get down to the business of being successful in a creative and interesting way. They are ready to listen, take on board new ideas, seek out opportunities and throw in a few surprises of their own.

They are whole people.

"The secret of the man who is universally interesting is that he is universally interested."
William Dean Howells

Interesting in the Kitchen

Long gone are the days when cookery programmes were just about recipes. Now it's much more interesting. It's very much the brand of the personality chef that we tune into. We still talk about the food, but it has become a lot more than that.

It was probably Graham Kerr the "Galloping Gourmet" that made us sit up and view cookery programmes as something more than a piece of mouth-watering enlightenment. We have become interested in the people behind the food. Food has been made very interesting by the interesting people who are cooking it. Would we be tuning in to write down the ingredients and instructions if we were not drawn to the person revealing their latest gastronomic delights? Possibly not.

Keith Floyd, a man whose list of ingredients would be as precise as to contain items such as "a load of eggs", was a pioneer of "chefstravaganza". His flamboyant, devil-may-care attitude captured the interest of viewers throughout the UK, giving rise to a great following of culinary disciples all eager to stamp their mark on the TV chef scene.

We are now treated to an absolute cornucopia of cooking madness, with crazy prof Blumenthal in his lip-smacking lab of weird creation, *Naked Chef* Jamie Oliver literally throwing food together for his cool mates. There's Ms Lawson smothering us with sumptuous portions of *Nigellissima*, and sweary-shouty, tell-it-as-it-is, who can I upset next... Gordon Ramsay making a nuisance of himself in other people's kitchens.

Showmanship to generate interest and seduce us into buying the books of the brands. Food for thought – yum yum!

Boo!

Surprise others and yourself.

If you're not **being** interesting, you're not really **being**

So what have we learnt about how to be interesting? Well, we have learnt a lot. We've gone from Plato and Socrates to phrenology and neuroscience with a lot of interesting diversions on the way.

We've picked the brains of some brilliant and interesting people. We've looked at ourselves and how we see the world. We've looked at how others see us.

This book started off as a vague idea. It then became an investigation – a series of questions and "what if?" thoughts. From these starting points it evolved into a voyage of discovery. A look at the elements that go to make that thing we call "being interesting". We're sure we've missed some by the way ....

This was never meant to be an instructional book. There are no hard and fast rules, no secret formulas and no magic key to How to be Interesting. But there are hundreds of things we can all do to help us be interesting. They are spread around this book and in the mind maps.

Most of them, if not all of them, we're sure you knew already. All we've done really is give some gentle reminders to take the time to explore some of them in a little more focus. We've intentionally gone out of our way to get you to think about what it means to "be interesting".

It seems to us that everyone can "<u>be</u> interesting". Because everyone is interesting. It's what makes human existence what it is.

To be interesting is an essential part of the human condition. 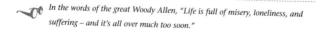 If we're not <u>being</u> interesting, we're not really <u>being.</u> And we must keep reminding ourselves that not to be interesting <u>is</u> a terrible waste. Everyone has a story to tell. Everyone is a story. Tell it. And tell it well.

If we set out to live an interesting life and be an interesting person, the first thing we have to do is start being interested in others and everything around us. That's a benefit in itself.

To be interesting we have to have a good work–life balance. That means allowing time for other interests, hobbies, sports, the arts, literature, music ….

To be interesting we have to be curious and learn to cultivate an enquiring mind with a healthy thirst for knowledge.

To be interesting we need to keep asking questions and looking for answers.

All of these are benefits in themselves. They will help us be happier, more rounded, more content individuals.

What's more these don't only benefit us as individuals. They benefit everyone around us and make the world a better place.

As Mr Spock of *Star Trek* would say: *"Dif-tor heh smusma."* That's "Live long and prosper" in Vulcan.

In the words of the great Woody Allen, "Life is full of misery, loneliness, and suffering – and it's all over much too soon."

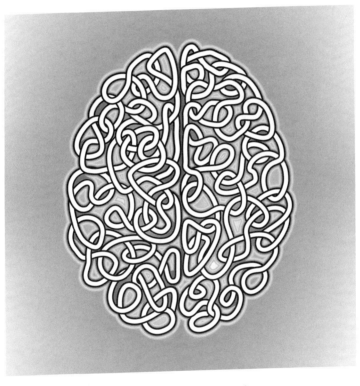

An interesting life is a fascinating journey.

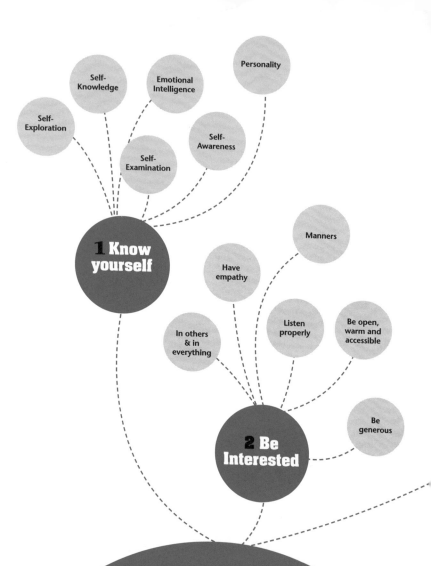

Self-Exploration

Self-Knowledge

Emotional Intelligence

Personality

Self-Examination

Self-Awareness

1 Know yourself

Have empathy

Manners

In others & in everything

Listen properly

Be open, warm and accessible

2 Be Interested

Be generous

How to be interesting

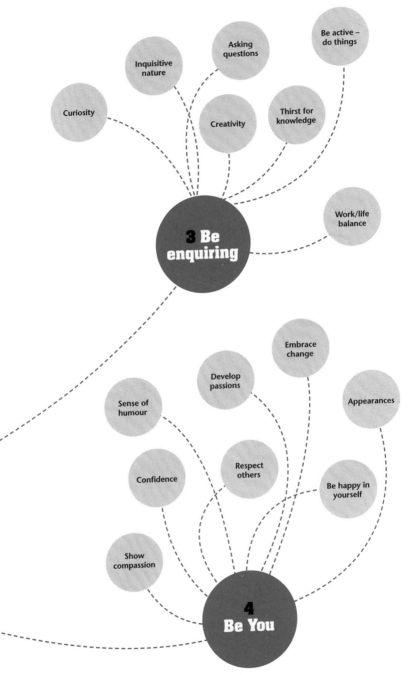

- Curiosity
- Inquisitive nature
- Asking questions
- Be active – do things
- Creativity
- Thirst for knowledge

3 Be enquiring

- Work/life balance

- Sense of humour
- Develop passions
- Embrace change
- Appearances
- Confidence
- Respect others
- Be happy in yourself
- Show compassion

4 Be You

INT.STUDY.DAY

Dave and Mark look at the finished mind map.

> DAVE
>
> That looks pretty complete to me.

> MARK
>
> I know.

> DAVE
>
> Anything we've missed?

> MARK
>
> Don't think so but you can't be sure can you?

> DAVE
>
> ~~No. Okay then. Well that looks like we've covered~~
> pretty much everything. I reckon we can finish
> ~~writing this book now.~~

> MARK
>
> Yeah. Why not?

> DAVE
>
> Hang on a mo. I've just thought of something else.

> MARK
>
> Me too.

Keep moving forward

To be interesting we must always be changing.

The most interesting man in the world?

The Argentine matinee idol, Fernando Lamas, might well have been the most interesting man in the world. He was certainly the inspiration behind the creation of that character for a Dos Equis beer campaign. The man playing the character in the ads is Lamas's close friend and American actor Jonathan Goldsmith.

The subject of this series of commercials is a suave, debonair older man in his 70s with a beard. He's called The World's Most Interesting Man.

The commercials show him performing outrageous, daring feats in exotic locations. Just a few of them include fighting Ninjas, bench-pressing two beautiful women, catching a marlin Hemingway-style, surfing a massive wave and freeing a Grizzly Bear from a vicious trap.

The voice-over to the commercials makes equally outrageous, bold and humorous claims – "if he were to punch you in the face, you would have to fight off the strong urge to thank him" ... "people hang on his every word, even the prepositions" ... "the police often question him because they find him so interesting" are just some of them. Others worth mentioning are "alien abductors have asked him to probe them"..."even his enemies list him as their emergency contact" and our favourite "he can speak French, in Russian".

Each commercial ends with the pay off – "stay thirsty my friends".

When the ad agency was asked to comment on its strategy it said: "He is a man rich in stories and experiences, much the way the audience hopes to be in the future. Rather than an embodiment of the brand, The Most Interesting Man is a voluntary brand spokesperson: he and Dos Equis share a point of view on life that it should be lived interestingly."

The success of the campaign has been huge. Goldsmith remembers being approached by a man in a restaurant who told him this little story.

When he had asked his young son what he would like to be when he grew up, his son had replied: "I want to be The Most Interesting Man in the World. Stay thirsty my friends."

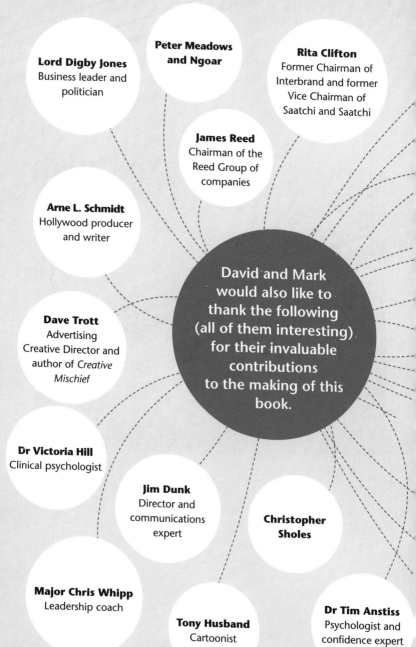

Lord Digby Jones
Business leader and politician

Peter Meadows and Ngoar

Rita Clifton
Former Chairman of Interbrand and former Vice Chairman of Saatchi and Saatchi

James Reed
Chairman of the Reed Group of companies

Arne L. Schmidt
Hollywood producer and writer

Dave Trott
Advertising Creative Director and author of *Creative Mischief*

David and Mark would also like to thank the following (all of them interesting) for their invaluable contributions to the making of this book.

Dr Victoria Hill
Clinical psychologist

Jim Dunk
Director and communications expert

Christopher Sholes

Major Chris Whipp
Leadership coach

Tony Husband
Cartoonist

Dr Tim Anstiss
Psychologist and confidence expert

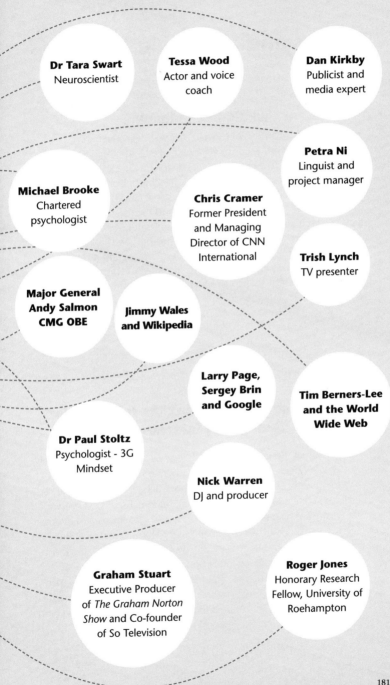

Dr Tara Swart
Neuroscientist

Tessa Wood
Actor and voice coach

Dan Kirkby
Publicist and media expert

Petra Ni
Linguist and project manager

Michael Brooke
Chartered psychologist

Chris Cramer
Former President and Managing Director of CNN International

Trish Lynch
TV presenter

Major General Andy Salmon CMG OBE

Jimmy Wales and Wikipedia

Larry Page, Sergey Brin and Google

Tim Berners-Lee and the World Wide Web

Dr Paul Stoltz
Psychologist - 3G Mindset

Nick Warren
DJ and producer

Graham Stuart
Executive Producer of The Graham Norton Show and Co-founder of So Television

Roger Jones
Honorary Research Fellow, University of Roehampton

Thanks and acknowledgements

Dave
would like to thank...

Biz, Gabbie, Saskia, Stuart, Maggie, Alex, Hannah, Lyla Greg and Maurice Gillespie; Julie Nixon, Alan Baker, Matt Kendall, Eddie Lee, Kelly Vance Dr Paul Stoltz, Bob Perry and Derek Arden; Stanley Jackson, JJ Jackson; Helen Filmer, Sue Grantly and all at JAA; Martin Sims, Jamie Grant, Julie Theivendran, Hannah Wilkinson, Alex Lynch White and the Earache crew; Alison Frecknall, Liz Mulkerrin, Dai Taylor, Bradley Honor, Lorraine Ellison OBE, Libby Sutcliffe, Sacha Maloney, Susan Turnbull, Sir Clive Woodward; Rashpal Parmer, Dennis Wren, Jennifer Suggate and all at Bowker Orford; Bruce Priday, Ray Burdis, Charles Parsons and Willie O'Neil; Georgie Gulliford, Melanie Jessop, Laura Jury, Annalie Wilson, Pat and Heather Abernathy, Dave Marsden, Susan Gibson, The Speechworks team and all at Spotlight.

Mark would like to thank the following for being very interesting...

Kate, Thomas, Benedict, Olivia. Pat, Jenny, and all the Warren family. The Blundens. The Rowans. St Catherine's Primary and Colfox schools. Betty Starkey. Royal Holloway College. Charles Peattie. Ian Hislop, Francis Wheen, Tony Rushton, Bridget Tisdall and everyone at *Private Eye* magazine. All the great actors, producers and directors I've worked with. Ali MacPhail, Henry Normal, and all at Baby Cow Productions. Jonathan Shipley, Jenny Ng, and all the team at Capstone. Russell Taylor. Simon Tidball. Nick and Petra. Chesil Beach. The River Thames. Brian Eno. Thomas Hardy. Bernie, Kent, June, Miriam and all at The Groucho Club. Colin and Bernadette. Crandon and Dorothy. Anne and Bernard. All at Spotlight. Everyone who works with The Speechworks and all our lovely clients.

Illustration and Image Credits

Pi, 5, 40, 83, 107, 176 Piece of lined A4 paper with aged effect and hole punch – Nicemonkey/ Shutterstock.com

Piv, 11, 13, 46 An icon set of doodled cartoon smiley faces in a variety of expressions – ARENA Creative/ Shutterstock.com

Pv Optical illusion created by clay columns forming shapes of two ladies talking – Juriah Mosin/ Shutterstock.com

Pvi Author photos www.daitaylor.co.uk and www.canarywharfphotography.com

P1, 7, 8, 10, 23, 25, 52, 88, 92, 122, 136, 138, 146, 155, 168 white ripped paper – Eky Studio/ Shutterstock.com

P4 Illustration of a new fridge on a white background – Fotovika/Shutterstock.com

P6 Closeup of a small porous stone gargoyle – JHDT Stock Images LLC/Shutterstock.com

P11 Road with sign pole and blue sky with clouds – Rihardzz/Shutterstock.com

P11 Blank green road sign – ponsulak/Shutterstock.com

P21 Bath sponge isolated on white background – Svetlana Lukienko/Shutterstock.com

P25 The statue of Plato at the facade of the Academy of Athens in Greece – The Crow/Shutterstock.com

P30 Type of personality in word collage – Nypokcik/Shutterstock.com

P33 Personality inventory listed on a blackboard – Christophe Jossic/Shutterstock.com

P45 Human colour brain isolated – i3alda/Shutterstock.com

P58 Vintage woman face pop art retro poster – Icons Jewelry/Shutterstock.com

P60–61 Silhouette of a head isolated on white background – Blueplanet/Shutterstock.com

P64 High quality traced posing people silhouettes – Malko/Shutterstock.com

P66 A brand new fridge – RetroClipArt/Shutterstock.com

P73 Head and brain gears in progress. concept of human thinking – VLADGRIN/Shutterstock.com

P76 Vintage tin sign – Open sign – Callahan/Shutterstock.com

P76 Retro vintage closed sign with grunge effect – Vintage vectors/Shutterstock.com

P77 The human ear vector – Thirteen-Fifty/Shutterstock.com

P80 Woman telling secrets, pop art retro style illustration – Lavitrei/Shutterstock.com

P89 Question mark made from colourful speech bubbles – Petr Vaclavek/Shutterstock.com

P92 Speech bubble with question mark icons – Marish/Shutterstock.com

P94 Business discussion – RetroClipArt/Shutterstock.com

P100 Mad scientist extending explosive concoction away from his face – Angie D'Amico/Shutterstock.com

P102 Retro poster with robot – Bananafish/Shutterstock.com

P106 Vector light bulb – Vector/Shutterstock.com

P109 Set of icons on a theme fish – Aleksander1/Shutterstock.com

P111, 172 Large, old style round glasses with very thick lenses – TerryM/Shutterstock.com

P114 Pin-up girl listen retro radio – Trifonova Anna/Shutterstock.com

P120 Lion Tamer – Dennis Cox/Shutterstock.com

P123 Photo supplied by Jenny Ng

P127 Chimpanzee drawing vector – ComicVector703/Shutterstock.com

P129 Presentation lady – RetroClipArt/Shutterstock.com

P135 Detailed black fingerprint isolated on white background – Phecsone/Shutterstock.com

P139 Hipster glasses, Hipster man – Sasha Chebotarev/Shutterstock.com

P141 A brand new suit – RetroClipArt/Shutterstock.com

P143 Couple enjoying magazine – RetroClipArt/Shutterstock.com

P145 Leonardo da Vinci (1452–1519) "Mona Lisa" La Gioconda. Reproduction from illustrated Encyclopedia "Treasures of art", Partnership «Prosvesheniye», St. Petersburg , Russia , 1906 –Oleg Golovnev/Shutterstock.com

P149 Radio announcer 2 – RetroClipArt/Shutterstock.com

P154 Graphic for time management – DeiMosz/Shutterstock.com

P155 Vector cinema icons: film reel, stack of reels, film strip and clapboard – YasnaTen/Shutterstock.com

P163 Very old face – very old photo – Zurijeta/Shutterstock.com

P164 Hand with pointing finger in black and white – ElenaMaria/Shutterstock.com

P173 Hand-drawn human brain, a thinking human concept – Plean/Shutterstock.com

P177 Head made of arrows – Aleksander1/Shutterstock.com

P179 Movie ending screen – Callahan/Shutterstock.com

Illustrations supplied by Tony Husband: pages viii, 12, 97, 99

Illustration supplied by Curtis Allen (www.curtisallen.co.uk): page 26

"Trust that little voice in your head that says 'Wouldn't it be interesting if...'; And then do it."

Duane Michals